Editorial

Perceptive readers will have noticed a better standard of production in this number of Chapman. Our old DTP system which served us well simply had to go. The problem, as ever, was finance. *Chapman*, both magazine and publications, while having to exist in the real world of commerce, are not fundamentally commercial propositions. Inevitably we have to rely much on goodwill: from writers, from readers, from staff and volunteers.

Scottish & Newcastle have an honourable record of sponsoring the arts. Of all the arts in Scotland, literature has perhaps been the most culturally enriching, yet it is difficult to raise sponsorship for it. In the world of literature there are few glittering occasions, press premieres etc. S & N have been one of the few to put funds into writing – they gave generous sponsorship to the Scottish Poetry Library in its first few years. I approached Alastair Mowat, managing director of Scottish & Newcastle, for help with updating our desktop publishing system – an enterprise otherwise beyond our means. He was immediately responsive, and S & N offered us £1,500 towards a new system, and gave us some surplus machinery. With this as a basis, we have been been able to begin the process of upgrading.

It gives me great pleasure to announce this sponsorship and to express our thanks to S & N for their sympathetic support. Our publications already look better as a result, and are easier to produce, enabling us to do much more. The upgrading process is not yet complete: we need another computer and a scanner and are currently seeking further help with this. If any reader can help, please get in touch.

This issue, at general election time, publishes Tom Nairn's essay updating his now legendary *Last Minister and the Last Sunday Post* 'joke'. It mirrors the new confidence and vibrancy evident in Scotland today and carries the debate forward. Our feature on Neil Gunn, looking back over the achievements of the centenary celebrations last year, offers an overview of the state of Gunn scholarship. It emphasises Gunn's backstage role in the nascent nationalist movement, and demonstrates that figures like T S Eliot were fully aware of the international importance of Gunn's writing.

Chapman has strongly advocated political autonomy for Scotland over the entire period of its publication. We have never advocated a particular party line, believing it is up to the people of Scotland to decide what degree of autonomy they wish to have. As I write the prospect looks encouraging: Gaelic is prospering; the Scots Language Resource Centre looks set fair to be established in Perth, and Radio Scotland's Scots Language Week has made an important start to giving Scots its proper place in the media.

Finally, I am sad to report the death of Janet Caird, one of our regular contributors. We will be looking at her work in a coming issue.

Scottish Identity: a Cause Unwon

Tom Nairn

You talked of Scotland as a lost cause and that is not true. Scotland is an *unwon* cause.   **– John Steinbeck, letter to Mrs John F Kennedy**

Joke History

This is the story of a Scottish (but non-Celtic) joke. Twenty years ago I wrote down what seemed then just a rhetorical, throwaway phrase:

Scotland will be reborn the day the last Minister is strangled with the last copy of the *Sunday Post*. I hope I'm not alone.

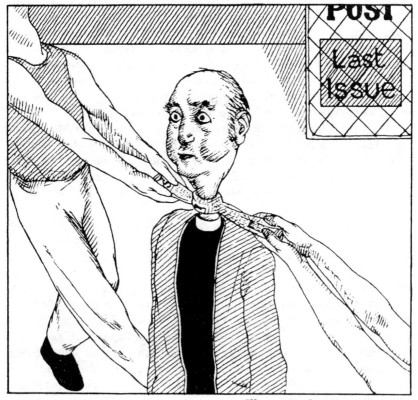

Illustration by Simon Manfield

These sombre words were published (not at all in a joking spirit) in 1970. They have reached maturity still alive, though somewhat transformed. The birth took place in a collection of essays edited by Karl Miller, *Memoirs of a Modern Scotland*. The literary source of my metaphor was the 18th century philosopher Diderot's idea that humanity would be freed when "the last king was strangled with the entrails of the last priest". Many readers will know the distinguished lineage of the phrase. Diderot got it, probably via Voltaire, from a French Minister, the militantly atheist priest Jean Meslier. In his infamous *Testament* he cites some "ignorant, uneducated fellow" who once told him that "all the great folk of the earth and nobles ought to be hung up and strangled with priests' guts".

The notion became popular among Enlightenment radicals, and was quoted and misquoted all over the place. So it was belatedly imported into Scotland in 1970. Though belated, the import became almost at once extremely popular. In the intervening years the idea has become oddly famous, and acquired a curious, almost folkloristic status – like a small emblem or national monument. The thieving common chord stole my intent. So it might be interesting to revisit the Last Minister now. His strange fate may even tell us something about an even stranger animal, 'Scottish Identity'; and it may even tell us something about what in that identity may have been changing since 1970.

The Last Minister is due a visit because he and his mysterious assailant have begun to haunt the author personally. Last year, I went to a reception for William Storrar's book *Scottish Identity: a Christian Vision*. Storrar is a latter-day Meslier, a youthful and recalcitrant Minister whose first book was a valiant attempt to navigate Presbyterianism into more militant support for the nationalist cause. The author told me, with the usual mischevious grin, that *Sunday Post*s would be handed out later, once those assembled – mainly men of the cloth – had had a few drinks and were ready for execution.

The joke has been translated into foreign languages, and now appears in at least one tourist guide to Scotland, Christian Civardi's *Ecosse*. It gets elaborated and parodied all the time. It has been made into cartoons, and one anonymous poem depicts the author as actually carrying out the deed. In this tartan joke-*Götterdämmerung* – "Oor Tammas, his hairt dirlin fast" races doon the carse to take care of the wretched McSloth, Scotland's last surviving pulpiteer. This "haverin glaverin man o the cloth" makes a run for it, but to no avail:

> the last *Sunday Post*
> He throttled the Rev'rend
> Till his een were crossed...

Joke-Identity?

So this cry of rage has turned into a national joke. But if Scotland was a country where Ministers and priests really did get strangled and shot for political reasons, there could of course be no joke. The idea acquired its fabular nature partly because Presbyterian Ministers – and whatever they stand for in Scottish culture – are in truth not only safe but unassailable. But they are also – all too easily – identified as the spiritual captains of our captivity. There have always been plenty of other, more fitting candidates for strangulation. The Last Big Landowner would still be popular in Highland Scotland. The Last Capitalist used to be popular in Glasgow, until the city became Europe's Cultural Capital last year and – to the regret of many – attempted to modernise its PR image. Few in Scotland would be heartbroken about the last Lord Advocate, or the last Regional Council Leader.

But none of these enjoy the special historical and political significance attached to the Presbyterian Church of Scotland, the Kirk's semi-identification with modern national history and the role of its annual General Assembly as a surrogate parliament. It's precisely because the Calvinist Kirk was as near as we got to popular democracy in our separate history as a nation that seeing Ministers as special agents of our Fallen state makes a crooked, dream-sense.

The last Scottish religious revolution took place in 1843, when part of the Scottish Church rebelled on democratic grounds against the British State's interference in religious matters, and withdrew to constitute a Free Kirk. But in spite of its democratic instincts, this "rebellion of the pious" was no political revolution. In fact it was transformed into a retreat from politics – an abandonment of the corrupt external universe for spiritual and homely values, for the small scale of individual or small-community morality. In the long run such quietism in turn made Ministers (whether Free or established) appear as a body to collude with the status quo, whatever their individual political views. Those who in the 16th and 17th centuries had overthrown monarchs were now telling people to stay home and read the *Sunday Post*.

We can now see more clearly what's happening in the myth-image. As Freud pointed out, jokes are close relatives of dreams. And here poetic dream-justice is being done to a symbolic culprit, with an instrument which represents the national popular culture he is seen as having fostered; one which represents the Scottish identity we actually do have as distinct from the nobler, more radical and inspiring personae we would like to have, and often pretend to have, notably in the presence of outsiders.

· So, one Scottish identity is being comically wished away, wiped off the map. But what about the rebirth – what is put in its place? Well, that depends on who the strangler is, or what he or she stands for.

Joke-Revolution

The strangler has to be some sort of revolutionary. A fantasy revolutionary, of course; but also one present in most Scots. What he expresses is clearly a cry of protest against pettiness, against the kitsch and complacent folksiness which McSloth and the instrument of his doom are supposed jointly to stand up for – "tartanry", to sum all that up – the degraded image in the national mirror.

There are innumerable literary expressions of this – the most obvious example being the entire work of 20th century Scotland's major man of letters, Hugh MacDiarmid. His life can be seen as a non-stop shriek of protest at that image, an unceasing guerilla war against his country's fallen state, conducted with a bewildering (and often contradictory) set of armaments. That *Drunk Man Looking at the Thistle* in the 1920s was almost any Scottish literary intellectual looking in the identity-mirror from then to the present.

But let's take a more recent example: William McIlvanney's short story 'Dreaming' (*Walking Wounded*). McIlvanney is best known for *Docherty*, a proletarian *Bildungsroman* of the 1970s, and 'Dreaming' is a miniature of the same themes, made into a film by BBC Scotland. Its hero is Sammy Nelson, a typical Scottish 17-year-old from the industrial West of Scotland, sent out by anxious but well-meaning parents to look for his first job. As he goes, he too can't help wishing away the real world, as violently as possible:

> Most of the people around him were all right. It was the circumstances of their lives that Sammy rebelled against, the greyness, the lack of horizons, the acceptance of whatever was given. Walking through the dull streets, Sammy became for ten minutes a revolutionary. El Nelsono would lead his people to freedom ... 40 million pesetas for the head of El Nelsono! But no-one would betray him...

Shortly after leaving the local offices of Strathclyde Regional Council – still jobless – he blows them up with an imaginary bomb. The rest of the story (and still more the film) is a series of similar 'Walter Mitty' incidents, in which various aspects of Scotland are annihilated and replaced with something better.

Or as another West of Scotland writer, Gordon Williams, put it unforgettably in a poem introducing his 1972 novel *Walk, Don't Walk:*

> We knew our country was a smalltime dump where nothing ever happened and there was nothing to do. And nobody had a name like Jelly Roll Morton.

So the tiny, violent image of the Last Minister's fate is part of a larger view, and a larger problem. At least once a day, most Scots want to strangle somebody – not just anybody, someone relevant to a communal, national sense of depression or frustration.

But who can this be? Now we know who the strangler is, it's obvious that he has attacked the wrong victims. Kirk Ministers and the *Sunday Post* cannot seriously be blamed for such recurrent frustration, for the unemployment figures, for such a massive chip on the Scottish shoulder. Rather than causes, they are symptoms of whatever is amiss with the "smalltime dump" identity. And in that case, who *should* the strangler have been finishing off?

Joke Nation?

Any outsider will see the paradox at once. The most significant thing is who is *not* being strangled: an Englishman. One would expect a nationalist joke-myth to do precisely that. But in fact this protesting revolutionary wanted to finish off certain native customs and attitudes – those things about ourselves which we just can't stand one minute longer, although we may have to stand them for the rest of our lives. This betrays something crucial about Scottish identity. Scotland is not a colonised culture, but a self-colonised one.

The Last Minister mini-drama caught on because it resumes both the humour and the anguish, not of any general dissatisfaction or oppression, but of this special sort of captivity. That is, of an oppression which – though real enough – has historically been largely self-inflicted and self-sustained. The Scots were not conquered, or forcibly assimilated. They conquered and partly assimilated themselves, over a remarkably long period of time for good reasons and opportunities, chances it appeared unreasonable for a small and marginal nation to refuse.

But at the same time they have always resented doing so. And over the last twenty years they have begun to resent it more and more, and tended more to dream of its destruction. This is the period in question, since Le Curé Meslier made his first formal bow of introduction – the era of rising political nationalism, demands for devolution or self-government and (most recently) the publication of the all-party *Scotland's Claim of Right* in 1988, and the establishment of the Scottish Constitutional Convention.

In Scotland, however, such resentment immediately encounters a peculiar obstacle. It is inevitably, and in a historical sense rightly, linked to self-hatred and a degree of self-disparagement. Unlike nearly all other colonised or forcibly assimilated peoples, the Scots really do have mainly themselves to blame, and so mainly themselves – or a part of themselves – to attack and destroy.

A chosen and sustained national servitude has rules quite different from those of classical colonialism. One of these should be borne in mind constantly, whenever a Scottish conversation turns towards politics. Self-colonisation is easier to put up with than the standard variety. People aren't imprisoned or shot, newspapers and languages are not suppressed (at least not explicitly in modern times), and metropolitan opinion regards one with indifference rather than racist hostility – an occasional nuisance rather than a foe of "all we hold dear".

This is easier to endure, but far, far harder to shake off. An internalised submission has turned people into their own jailers who have locked up their own will-power, their capacity for collective purpose and action. This blockage is the real knot the central nexus – of Scottish identity. And the last two decades have demonstrated just how hard it is to untie. Another of the rules is the internalisation of duality. All dependency of one people on another creates a duality, obviously. The subordinate or marginalised community has both to try to remain itself on the one hand, and to live with the dominant state on the other. In that sense, identity-dilemmas being pulled two ways at once – are a commonplace feature of dependency. Or, put more solemnly, that Scottish identity became locked into roguery, ambivalence and double-facing or double-edged dilemmas of many different kinds.

Une nation sans état (to use the term of Jacques Leruez) could only survive by institutionalised duplicity, by canny manoeuvres along the ever-shifting, slippery path between autonomy and assimilation. Such stratagems of servitude compose the greater part of what passes for 'politics' in Scotland. These have been well chronicled in a book by one of Scotland's few Conservative intellectuals, Michael Fry, called *Patronage and Principle: A Political History of Modern Scotland* (1987). The title is naturally ironic. There are no principles in Scottish politics *proprement dit* – only forms of patronage, or generally futile (though occasionally noble) protests against it.

It is hardly surprising, then, that this overarching game which has determined the general trajectory of Scottish affairs since the mid-18th century should have generated so many other games in its wake. I suspect that's what Edwin Muir really meant in his oft-quoted 1941 poem about Scotland as a "joke nation" the nation which "never really means it", and prefers to pass off its suffering as humour.

My thesis is indeed that elective servitude has over this long period of time generated an entire cultural support-structure. This culture – being precisely "cultural" and often outward-looking in its aspiration – is often unaware of its true function. That function can't be simply categorised – it is neither colonial nor nationalist in the usual sense. It has elements of both of these. But, essentially it echoes that odd, very *sui generis* structure I mentioned before: the chosen, balanced equivocation of self-colonisation.

The Scottish-Jewish Joke

Returning now to that mini-psychodrama of the Last Minister. Why was it considered so funny? Comic, rather than pathetic or sad, like so many Scottish identity manoeuvres? As with most aspects of Scottish nationality and nationalism, perspective is difficult. However, one might to look at it as a kind of Jewish joke. In *Jokes and Their Relation to the Unconscious*, Freud points out how the effect of much old (pre-Israeli) Jewish humour was really to divert and defuse aggression, so that life could go on. Jews told stories against themselves for that very reason – "tendentious jokes" is Freud's term for them: A particularly favourable occasion for tendentious jokes (he goes on) is presented when the intended rebellious criticism is directed against the subject himself, or against someone in whom the subject has a share – a collective person, that is (the subject's own nation, for instance).

Jewish anti-Jewish jokes rehearse the same sparky rebelliousness found in so much Scottish humour, the same nagging discontent with captivity and dependency. And also the same wry resignation: the shrug of the shoulders once the laughter is over. Freud shows how the practical point of Jewish humour was often that of a safety valve – both to exhibit protest and to reconcile the captive community with its lot.

"Incidentally," Freud sighs, near the end of this chapter on 'The Purpose of Jokes', "I do not know whether there are many other instances of a people making fun to such a degree of its own character…" Well: there is at least one. And for reasons oddly parallel to those of the pre-*Shoah* Jews, who were also captives of the greater cultures and states around them, also colluded in and ably exploited such dependency, while continuing to resent and fear it.

There too political quiescence, paralysis of the communal will, was (until the birth of Zionism) habitually chosen – almost instinctively adhered to – as the safer course. And the results Freud underlines – a humour of self-diminution, where self-hatred vies with compensatory self-assertion – are about equally visible in the two situations. The forever struggling small man of Jewish tradition, most famous in 20th century form as Charlot and Woody Allen, has his obvious counterpart in the Glasgow "wee bauchle" constantly and spiritedly fighting back against defeat and humiliation, but never really winning. At the present moment he is represented by Gregor Fisher's Rab C Nesbitt. The point of the double-entendre is the same, and is also famously visible in the chronicles of the 19th century Scottish music-hall, in many ancestral images of empty truculence and wild Caledonian hilarity. These are normally followed by a kind of implosion – all-round collapse into the 'black hole' of Caledonian despond, that frightful sense of paralysis and doom where so many of our identity-games (and our political conversations) end up.

We are returned to Sammy's grey streets and the lack of horizons, to a reality felt as immutable. Something inside us will go on despising it – something fortified by the flash of liberatory fantasy. But something else inside us embraces the greyness, the sense of castration, and – in Scotland at least – usually with a definite degree of masochism.

In McIlvanney's story this is put into the mouth of the local government bureaucrat ("That's the real world out there … You're going to have to learn … Work, effort, sheer effort…" and so on). But of course people older than Sammy learn to tell themselves all this. The transformation of reality into fate: the meaning is always really a destiny unalterable by us alone – *sìnn féin* – by our own separate political will.

Joke Dividedness

I can't begin to describe all the identity-games and *döppelgangers* infesting the Scottish psyche. Just listing them would take up an article in itself. But there is one about which it is necessary to say something: – the larger historical joke typified by the literary "Antisyzygy". This monster is regrettably familiar to you all. A classical pedigree is provided by Alan Bold in his short study of Modern Scottish Literature (1983).

> Scottish Literature shows the various ways that the Scottish people live with
> the pressure and persistence of the past ... Defeat is a divisive issue and division
> is responsible for the state of Scotland ... Division is more than a physical
> presence, it is a mental condition. It can even be a pathological condition as in
> Stevenson's *The Strange Case of Dr Jekyll and Mr Hyde* (1886), which
> contains, or rather reveals, the classic artistic image of internal division.

Scottish writers have naturally had as an aim "to piece together the fragments of defeatism in a healing image of artistic wholeness". But they have a lot to contend with, notably the Caledonian Antisyzygy (courtesy of G Gregory Smith, 1919) the notion that contradictoriness or a clash of extremes were inseparable from the Scottish psyche. Smith thus furnished a general cultural motif which has, alas, lasted almost to the present. It was (in Bold's words again) "the text for the secular sermon in which MacDiarmid announced the Scottish Renaissance".

That sermon long outlasted the Scottish Renaissance in any specific sense, in fact, to become something like a prevailing cultural assumption. In the 1960s it received psychiatric canonisation from the Glasgow therapist and sage R D Laing. One feature of Laing's work is what could be called the universalisation of the Antisyzygy – the depiction of a universe gloomily haunted by dividedness, in which all nations and individuals turn out to be as unlucky as the Scots. Thus parochial ill-fortune turns into a global malady of alienation, of splits between 'outer' and 'inner', across which the spirit shuttles forever to and fro – rather as MacDiarmid did, on that well-trodden, almost concreted path between Langholm and the Absolute, or between Auchtermuchty and the longed-for "eternal mood".

The Last Minister erupted first in *Memoirs*, as I mentioned, edited by the Scottish literary critic Karl Miller. It is relevant to notice that the joke was baptised and consecrated by someone who, in the intervening years, has made himself a world authority on doubleness. In an extensive study called *Doubles* (1985) Professor Miller also projects Scottish Angst upon the stars, revealing a brooding cosmos across which the reader is inxorably pursued by James Hogg's Robert Wringhim.

We meet him first as Miller's own schizophrenic aunt, "not altogether in touch with her whereabouts", and believing she's "two people rolled up into one"; and end up with the old scoundrel (so to speak) in the pulpit of St Giles' Cathedral, hammering the message home:

> Duality is departure and return. It is theft and restitution. It is megalomania and
> magnanimity. It is weakness, illness and illusion ... it courts and contemplates
> uncertainty, vacancy, doubt, dizziness, and arrest ... Very many other things,
> very many orders of thing, can be said with reference to duality...

Yes indeed. Scottish intellectuals are not just tiresomely but wilfully obsessed with duality. They never stop writing books, poems and great Scottish novels about it.

Parodying Professor Miller a little, one might reply that duality as a belief-system, a view of the world, is a way of appearing to make immense journeys while going nowhere at all. *Le nomadisme écossais* (a term not without some *retentissement* in contemporary French culture) is the most refined technique of armchair travel yet discovered, which could only have originated in a culture unable to travel other than in circles, and compelled, therefore, to pretend that the universe is itself circular.

Beyond a Joke

I have no space to do more than mention others, like the celebrated joke of the forged Celtic Passport, or the geographical antizyzygy of East versus West, Edinburgh versus Glasgow, *Fragmentosis Caledonica* etc. The point is, all these have a cultural function distinct from the intention behind them, and similar to that of our assorted psychodramas of split personality and doubleness. These are all identity-games which both express and limit effective protest at the captive condition of the Scots. And the vital limit is always political. It invariably has the sense of "we don't really mean it". Though sometimes this decodes as "we can't mean it ... because we have no self-confidence". We lack the self-confidence to act, rather than go round in identity-circles. The complaint normally implies that we can't act because we have a divided, sickly or two-headed "identity", because nature or – as Bold argues – a very ancient history, has made us the tragic world leaders in communal schizophrenia, as well as in heart disease and lung cancer.

Actually, I believe that nature has nothing to do with it, and religion and Ministers remarkably little. The truth is the other way round. Today's Scottish identity has all these neurotic traits because it won't act – because it entered a mainly political pact with the Anglo-British Devil and renounced separate existence as a state. From that disposition there has come a still-born or deadened dimension to our identity. It started in an age when politics were separate from culture and daily living. As Scottish society was modernised and that ceased to be true, the paralysis has crept into and affected everything.

The Scots feel they cannot act ('get it together', protest effectively) because they are forever in two minds. Actually, they're forever in two minds because they are unable to act having renounced the relevant means of action, and failed (so far) to generate a movement reclaiming those means. After 1746 and the military repression following Culloden this chosen bondage was not – did not need to be – maintained by force. Instead, it was reproduced by what I referred to earlier as stratagems of servitude, in both the administrative and the cultural arenas. Between the 1820s and the 1920s self-colonisation generated a formidable cultural and ideological apparatus – inevitably, a great part of what people today can't help meaning and referring to when Scotland's "identity" is mentioned.

The history of how this machinery of cultural collusion and servitude was built up is strangely unknown. What seems to be missing is a real history of the intellectuals in modern Scotland. I mean "the intellectuals" in the broader sense which would examine how the "thinking class" (the higher-educated, teachers, scientists, clerics, administrators and lawyers, as well as poets and prophets) has evolved. What we don't know much about is the history of *les intellectuels* in that wider, more functional sense. Scotland has always had a prominent institutional middle class. It overproduced "intellectuals" in the 19th century, in the most marked distinction to England. Its overall class structure remains to this day remarkably configured in that direction – and yet, we know all too little about the phenomenon. The one area where serious work has been done here is on the Enlightenment. Anand Chitnis and Richard Sher (for example) have given us some sense of ideas and ideologies in that era. Later on, however, there is very little. One has soon to look back to Henry Thomas Buckle's *History of Civilisation in England* (1857) with its important chapter on Scottish culture.

In other words, the theme has to be much deepened and farther pursued. This may be the one most pertinent to a better understanding of contemporary Scotland. And it may also be something particularly suitable for studying from a vantage-point outside the country itself – from the wider and more naturally comparative angle of "Scottish Studies" abroad. At Grenoble, or Mainz, or elsewhere, might it not in practice be easier to establish such a perspective upon Scottish culture?

Joke-nation status is really no joke. It requires intensive high-cultural and media labour to keep it going – (not only the *Sunday Post*), the letter-pages, the small magazines, or watching television. We aren't yet at the day when the old schizophrenia will burn down of its own accord. Nor can we hope to sing, write, or film our way out of it. The Scottish (and Gaelic) cultural renaissance of the 1980s has certainly altered the climate of Scotland in ways more favourable to escape. Just as its Ministers are no longer mainly quietist, so its intellectuals are no longer apologists of safely universal and abstract causes. Yet these tendencies will only last and bear the fruit they promise if a decisive political exit is found. Because Scottish identity's original weakness is on the political level – in the stillborn side of our collective awareness – it is that level alone which can supply an answer. The lack of confidence, the passivity and fragmentation – even the nihilism – produced by self-colonisation can only be got rid of by a common purpose.

In one of the few studies made of specifically political identity, the author came to a similar conclusion. He was a Scot, W J M Mackenzie, driven to the topic by the usual mixture of personal and national exasperation. His book *Political Identity* (1978) is, of course, a minefield of jokes. However, he emerges from them with this definition:

> The best formula I can find [to isolate political from other kinds of identification] is that of "common purpose" ... The political "great books" are about communality, about social entities, only to the extent that they are or may be capable of purposive communal action ... A discussion of political identity

is primarily a discussion of the conditions in which it is possible to realise "common purpose" . . .

I hope Mackenzie would be pleased by the big steps forward Scotland has recently made toward common purpose and the agreed resumption of a separate political identity. I certainly am. People have accused me of over-absorption in all the dubious dilemmas of Schizoland, as if I had made a trade out of them ("cottage industry" was one recent phrase used in this connection) and suggested I would face unemployment if Scottish neuroses were cured.

Nothing could be more untrue. The absolutely welcome truth to me is that Scotland will truly be reborn the day it stops laughing about the strangling of the last Minister, and begins to forget both about him and the *Sunday Post*. And about tragic dividedness, tartanry, and all the other alibis of inaction which have kept us within a ghetto of our own construction. Actually, I think it's because that day is fairly near that the old myth has recently been resurfacing so much.

It's really up to Sammy, in that McIlvanney story I quoted above. In the old days he would have been ground down in turn, and become just like the parents he loves, and can't stand. They and the old town are Scotland (or "Scottish identity") itself:

> In some ways he loved this grotty old town. Dingy though it was, especially in the rain and it rained often enough, it wound itself round your bones. It was the people, Sammy decided. He liked the people . . . even his father who sometimes appeared to have taken a degree in grumpiness ... His father was all right. Most of the people around him were.It was the circumstances of their lives that Sammy rebelled against...

These circumstances have changed a lot, but not yet enough. Enough, however, for it to be a lot clearer that he doesn't have to go on putting up with them. In the old days – the days of the Last Minister – Sammy would either have found himself one day sitting down to read the *Sunday Post* and snarling at his own children about the real world, or else become some kind of nomad – taken the road of spiritual or physical exile. "You talked of Scotland as a lost cause," wrote the American author John Steinbeck to Jacqueline Kennedy, "and that is not true. Scotland is an *unwon* cause."

In his day, I believe that Sammy will finally win it.

Tom Nairn

Peter Mowat

White Man With Daffodils In A Clear Glass

My window being half open
to the world,
my life having reached Thursday afternoon
with only superficial bruising,
I had turned Webern's Three Pieces for Orchestra up
as loud as I dare bearing in mind
my brother the man in the street's
dislike of anything beautiful, difficult and strange, when

bugger me if a black-hearted gull didn't do his business
on the windowsill from an altitude of ninety feet.

There's gratitude for you

Part Song

My mother hid her beauty,
the easy kind you hardly know is there,
not seen or heard, that rare.

Her instinct ran clean and true, a solid line of descant,
the lesser part in part song, the and of heaven and hell,
the beaten heart beating, the leavening of daily bread.

Glad and good can be without knowledge
of love. My father went to sea. We watched for him
sometimes on Friday. Monday nobody noticed him go.

I never saw my mother's beauty, not in her few dark
or brightest days. Maybe my children will see
clearly through my half-light in their own good time.

Drumtochty Shifts

Her trees are language rooted deep in this and other time.
They speak wood. They do not speak of wood. They speak wood.
Listening is hard. Sap runs unseen, and sings; it sings of silence.

Leaves come and go, buds burst. Drumtochty shifts in light as light
itself shifts, over time. The peace in her unease releases slow
green sensing, pulsed all through with brown, iconic reason, the
whys a fruit should utter, cry-sweet, bitter-loud, hurt made bright.

The other trees were sentences of life, centuries of structure,
surrounding crowds of sound, splintering meaning from slab dark
uproot lifeless words, winding, branching, choking each other, till

day of day returns and this cool burns. Her season uproots in us,
unripened, the whole blind half-life, what is left when heart unhealed
is only core, a latent birth, radiant in decay, the inside uttering.

And this is some of what I know, the peeled white bark has ripped,
her name all green with moss grown over, my skin roughed smooth on
memory - the time we can grasp is shabby. The city street is full
of empty rhymes, but the silences of trees and of love never leave us.

Catterline - The Marking Of Time

Divers bob black skulled, all
sleek among the seals; under lean of hull
a tideline splatters spare apparatus, bomb
gas bottles, sunken limpet, bared tuber roots.

Highbrow crown wide orphaned cottage eyes
hard hug their bay; shingle fleck is spittle sucked
through seascummed rocks - this sunlit sea-life lust
is innocent, the sudden planet impulse not yet cold.

An absolute displacement, the instinct mind
that turns us inside out, changing nothing.
How perfectly we fit this small diminishing of
history, her ribbed stone, the bleached bone.

*

Against the north earth heaves her flank, rubs unashamed
against the running channel; unsung fingers stretch to span
the still content spirit, the tidal grey, the lung's billow.

My chilren play at being alive; I am the waiting moment that marks
their time as they offer up a centimetre crab to the light, till it
slips through all our safety nets of fingers, words and place.

The soft shell may heal, will heal, I lie and
half believe myself; the fossils we lay down are evidence
not that life once lived but that emptiness will survive..

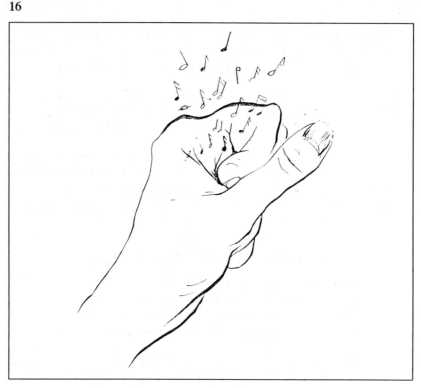

Illustration by Kirsten Harris

Song For My Daughter

My body is a hand
upon this instrument, the world.

Learning to play is coming
to terms with the chaos of our silence
in one out of only a hundred different ways.

This hand that is hard and knotted
is the bared tree branch
that winter leaves behind.

Rocks and stones have the sweetest music,
clean and clear as the early air;
its beauty is as simple and certain as pain.

I will not make sense of the world, or break it into seasons;
your song will have rhythms and unreasons of their own.

Peter Mowat

A Tale of Four Nations

Bernard Crick

"I am a citizen of a state with no agreed colloquial name." So I began both a recent essay in the Irish Review and an article in a memorial volume to the Ulster poet and critic, John Hewitt. Never waste a good phrase nor abandon a creative dilemma. I reflected on the difficulty we Brits (to use an Aussie expletive now favoured by both persuasions in Northern Ireland, where both Scots – sorry – and Welsh are "Brits" too) have in responding to the peremptory "Nationality?" in a foreign hotel register. Few people, I observe, write "British"; most mistakenly take the question literally, not as asking for one's legal citizenship. The question was framed not for us UKanians but for those in what are held to be normal, happy lands where one nation is one state (or so it is believed) but that belief is in itself a nationalist assumption, and obsession. The word "British" doesn't, to paraphrase Catullus, "warm the blood like wine", as "Scottish", "Welsh" and "Irish" do, and "English" can. "British is best" sounds to my ear either commercial or evasive of the question of identity. Those who write "citizen of the United Kingdom" are invariably Ulster loyalists, occasionally an aggressively pedantic Scottish Tory. But John Hewitt stubbornly believed himself to be of Ulster, of Ireland, and of Britain; and all the better for it. God knows what he wrote in the register.

The majority of British citizens write "English" in the register for the good enough reason that they are English. But many do so in the mistaken belief that "English" is the adjective corresponding to "citizen of the United Kingdom of Great Britain and Northern Ireland". The full title of the Union is a mouthful, and it has been appropriated by a party who no longer believe in a union of nations but in a central unified state, what some Victorian imperialist publicists called "Greater England". One needs a sense of history to digest the meaning of "United Kingdom". But many Englishmen and women, high and low, now seem to have lost just such a sense of history, are only left with a vague, warm, nostalgic and muddled mental mist called "English Heritage". Even to speak of "The Union" could risk, in some contexts, sounding either anti-Catholic or opposed to a Parliament in Scotland. But is too true a description of our modern history to surrender to partisan rhetoric? I am a democratic socialist, but if public political banquets were still the fashion, I would lift my glass, like a true Whig, and drink "to the Union, God bless it!" (although not if construed to favour the surrender of the Parliament of Scotland in 1707 or Ireland in 1800). In other words (if you want to know), I am some kind of federalist, even confederalist.

At the heart of the matter there is (what Mrs Thatcher could never grasp, or only in an English context) national feeling, indeed nationalism. But nationalism does not necessarily imply political separation, or mean that for each nation there must be a state. There are many multi-national states and there are also many areas of the world where political nationalism (Ireland, or Israel/Palestine, South Africa, Yugoslavia or "Greater Russia") is part of the problem, not of any "solution": a word like "resolution" is usually wiser.

The relationship between culture and politics is not as clear cut as most Nationalists believe. Our sense of identity may or may not need a separate state. We may or may not be better governed by a separate state; and where a sense of national cultural identity is already strong political separation may not make, either in economic or cultural terms, those dramatic differences that some hope for and others fear. Also the degree of independence possible in the modern interdependent world of nominally sovereign separate states is likely to be less than protagonists imagine. "Independence in Europe" to some is a genuine aspiration, to others a clever *sluaghghairm*; to a few a sell-out. But from the sidelines it seems to me to be in part at least a kind of realism, a recognition of the impossibility of standing alone, except at a price too high to pay, both economically and culturally; even if the realism only looks East and not South or immediately West, tries hard to ignore the historically entangled English and Irish connections.

Even after an independent Scotland, the English language will still bind the four nations as much as sustained episodes of English misgovernment have divided. The nationalist poets and novelists still read each other, and not just between the three nations: the English reader is still the largest audience for them all and English writers are still as much influenced by the three as the three are by them. Realistic nationalists can accept inter-relationships; but obsessional or fanatic nationalists believe that all influences are one-way, destructive, colonialist. I just mildly observe that the English language is not an instrument monopolised by the Tory Party, but the common property, with so many good regional variations, of all who use it and have used it to good effect. Even in Wales (Dylan Thomas's "two tongued sea") the speaking of Welsh is maintained, even slightly extended among intellectuals, at the price of abandoning, whatever Plaid Cymru's rhetoric, realistic separatist aspirations. (Quite simply, there is a large non-Welsh-speaking but nonetheless Welsh majority who will not have compulsory bilinguality forced upon them; and the special position of the language in schools was a pre-emptive political compromise instituted by English Tory leaders and dependent on Westminster.)

Many Scots, like many Welsh, have a vivid sense of dual identity, and for most purposes live with it comfortably, more so than most people in Northern Ireland, and find an enhanced quality of life in being able to live in two worlds, enjoy two cultures and their hybrids. But they perceive this as being Scottish and *British*, not Scottish and *English*. The late John Mackintosh made a similar point well in 1977:

The case for devolution explicitly limits political change to the level which allows self-awareness but excludes nationalist extremism. It keeps Scotland in the United Kingdom on the explicit grounds that Scots have a dual nationality ... Though this does not rule out the less pleasant forms of nationalism, it prevents the practical expression of any Scottish national feeling in the form of hostility to the English.

Is it this that is now being called into question? Even Mackintosh would occasionally slip into saying "English to express part of that dualism rather than what he plainly meant, "British". "British" does not, to my ear, convey a whole identity, like "Scottish" or "English", but simply the political elements of the culture, both customs and institutions, which are shared in common between the four main regions of the United Kingdom. Most Scots, I suspect, still have a dual nationality in those terms, Scottish and British, not Scottish and English. The question is complicated in every instance, but the distinction is reasonably clear; and not drawing it leads to much confusion. To be Welsh and British, for instance, need raise no *a priori* fears of Anglicisation, but to say "Welsh and English" does. Much of the sub-text, I suspect, of Scottish constitutional nationalism is an implicit comfortable comparison with Northern Ireland. Both separatists and devolutionists in Scotland can pursue a political path to somewhat different ends because, they feel, those ends are not so different as in Northern Ireland, nor do they inherit a living tradition of violent rather than political resolutions. But this does depend on how both sides behave. The English provocations or insensitivities of the 1960s and 1970s, when Mackintosh wrote, were of a kind more easily discounted than the confrontational, stridently Unionist politics of today's Conservative Party when faced with demands for Scottish home rule. Could Mackintosh speak as reasonably today as he did 20 years ago?

... two ways in which one can feel Scottish and I think I have experienced both. One ... is to feel a resentment against the assumptions of superiority, of absolute standards, so evident in the older English universities, in London media circles, among Whitehall civil servants and so on. The other, when one has been in and through all these groups and their activities, is to be reasonably confident that the best of what is done in Scotland and by Scots is as good as anything these guardians of proper standards can produce.

But this reasonable sense of dual identity is not shared by most English politicians today. It depends on historically sensitive behaviour towards the other nations in the Union, on the English majority not misusing their constitutional power and being misled by the dated doctrine of the sovereignty of Parliament.

This power has been abused and a constitutional crisis is looming, however little this is discussed south of the border due to the appalling under-reporting of Scottish politics and opinion in the London Media until the "fifty percent for separation" poll of early February 1992. Editors and political writers read the press wires for events in foreign countries, but they think they know all about Scotland already; but their knowledge is, in fact, a knowledge of political opinion in London gleaned from daily talk with people in London. They meet Scottish Labour and SLD MPs, of course, but they think they are exaggerating; and the Scots go home at weekends and in the recess, so are not much present on the London scene.

Yet was there ever a time (since the days of Walter Scott) when Scottish novelists, poets, painters and actors were held in higher esteem on the London scene, and recognised as distinctively Scottish? This may be wholly due, of course, to their intrinsic merits. But to hear SNP intellectuals and their literary fellow-travellers go on, the prejudiced English would be incapable of such objectivity. Perhaps the answer is a more subtle criticism of the Southern scene, about which I've ranted elsewhere: the separation of politics and literature – in England one has to go back to the 1930s (perhaps the myth of the 1930s) to find political intellectuals or "political writers" in Orwell's double sense (writers who tried, like him, to make "political writing into a work of art", and literary writers who are not politically illiterate).

One feature of an aroused nationalism is that writers and artists become interested in public questions, and may often have more influence, albeit indirectly, on the general state of public opinion than politicians and political editors. I would only add the important caveat that politics is not simply a world of commitment to strong convictions, but also deals with moral dilemmas, calling for empathic understanding of the clash of values and interests when each are equally justifiable to the protagonists. A writer may take sides, but always with reservations. Orwell once said that "a writer can never be a *loyal* member of a political party". There is even a discourse of imaginative speculation about politics rather than imaginative arguments. Think of Yeats. He could speak in both voices; or of John Arden, less fortunately: compare the Arden of *Armstrong's Last Night*, a real drama of real dilemmas, with the strident, stereotyped nationalist ranter of *The Ballygombeen Bequest*. Bad politics and bad theatre for the same reason: one-dimensional. Long ago Camus remarked of the Algerian crisis that it was not the business of intellectuals to find justifications for rival violence, but to seek to comprehend – a part of conciliation. There is a lot of waste ground to cultivate between the ivory tower and the trenches.

What is odd about English intellectuals is that they are still, with few exceptions, so a-political. This may be because, I seriously believe, they have not come to terms with their own nationalism. So much English nationalism is tacit, repressed, and the worse for that. I have read too often Scottish writers and critics who should know better, even Tom Nairn, even Cairns Craig, having a go at all English intellectuals for being neo-colonialist, somehow fundamentally inauthentic even as writers. They would do better to encourage English writers to show more interest in their own obvious Englishness, just as Scottish, Welsh and Irish writers are proudly and contentiously interested in their distinctiveness. To be very brief, the theory and doctrine of toleration (the degree to which we accept things from which we differ or disapprove) necessitates both knowledge of the others and *self*-knowledge.

Until the English come to terms with themselves as English, not as the only true British, they will not deal sensibly with "the others". Emyr Humphreys once wrote to me that he wasn't in the least upset at Orwell having nothing to say about Wales, rather he was grateful to find one English writer who was explicit and interesting about Englishness. But I think "the others" are at times to be faulted for pretending that national cultures are self-sufficient (give or take a tip of the hat to a vague-enough "Europe") and, in the peculiar case of the British Isles, not very much influenced by each of the others. Philip Dodd was more perceptive when he called "Englishness" a relationship. Because historically the numerically, politically and militarily dominant nation in the islands, England's own national characteristics are very much a product of an interplay with the others. In politics this is very clear. From the deposition of the Stuarts in 1688 until the separation of Eire in 1920, the main business of English politics was the holding together of the United Kingdom. The old Tories used to know that. When Kipling spoke of "the great game" he did not just mean the holding of the overseas Empire together. Celtic nationalist literature portrays the English, of course, as oppressors; but historians paint a much more complex picture of party divisions and of spasmodic cycles of conciliation and coercion in Ireland; and of deliberate policies of conciliation in Scotland after, but only after, the destruction of the Highland clan system in its military and economic aspects. In India the Raj did not practice "divide and rule", they ruled through existing divisions. To the disgust of liberals, they did not seek to reform them. It was a relative tolerance, certainly (as de Tocqueville saw) when contrasted to French imperial policies, the uniform system of administration, *la mission civilisatrice.*

But this is also true of culture. To be clear about our own identities, we need to know those of the others. Mutual influences are quite inseparable, even though they have not led to an homogenising Anglicisation or gentrification. By all means let us each be on our guard, but not always.

Yourselves of *Chapman, Planet* in Wales and *The Irish Review* comprehending North and South, each, of course, must look to their own, and do so well. But is there not some need to stimulate English writers and thinkers to join a broader dialogue, both cultural and political, about the nature of these islands, their interrelationships as well as their – at times angry, but sometimes highly respectful – differences? It sounds as if I am nerving myself to try to found a new political and cultural monthly, now that there can be some discussion of the interrelations of politics and literature in good plain English not dominated by Marxist narcissism (remember all that "the problem that nationalism poses for Marxism" stuff?). If so I will call it *The Four Nations Review.*   **Bernard Crick**

Sebastian Barker

Six Sonnets

I

What raptures in a woman's body, see, she breathes
Oceans of containment, sucking my index finger,
The intelligence of the world her eyes, the rest the waves
Of scampering knowledge seeking to understand her.

Liquid with authority, the lazy miracles roll
In beads of sweat and tears down her enormous smile,
While I, shaking from the shock of knowing so much, hold
Eternal form before the time of the sundial.

She blinks so slowly, I could compose a book
Before an eyelash returns to where it started.
She touches with such eloquence, believe me, were I blind,

I could read the scripture of her naked look.
No man may feel her fingers and hope to find
In the paradise of woman mankind brokenhearted.

II

We scent the sweetness tender as the trees'
Brave young leaves breathing an infinite wind.
For this is courage, the trust in all that frees
Purpose in life from the all-embittering mind.

Tendrils of praise, our fingers cradle buds,
Our darlings of the moment, as in our arms
We taste the spring we are through parted lips
Feasting on flesh the common sunshine warms.

We stop and sit and sip white wine and talk.
There's much too much to say, yet speech is heard
Praising the day we learnt one simple word

Culled from oblivion redeems. We name with ease
The blossoms we would die for, the erupting trees,
As arm in arm together we resume our walk.

III

Joy of my days, delight of my nights, hard partner
Walking the long paving-stones of Chelsea Embankment,
The sparkling light dandles on the grey river
The first principle of our love's bedazzlement.

You are no lady pricing the golden air,
Nor priceless statue turning in a glass museum,
For we've become one light, this light we share
Dancing the global stone through hand-held heaven.

Conspiracy of spring, behold in her
The green and lush amazement of yourself,
For you are what she is, this bed unfolding

Out of the black catastrophe of nightmare.
Redressed in clothes she hands me, I am the wealth
The rich aspire to in their tallest building.

IV

Jesus Christ it's horrible this pain
Invisible to doctors or the good,
For I am on the rack of what I am
Stung by the redhot pokers of her blood.

Though God I love, though sex I praise, though life
Is troubled not at all by what it kills,
I'll take this ghastly torture in my stride
And teach myself what loving woman means.

This dreadful wine, this cigarette on fire
With smoke I suck to stem my fever's flow,
Cannot control the madness I adore,

The loving of her supernatural soul.
She beats my broken brains, my body's all,
As, stung by love, I taste the love I know.

V

Serene, o moon, you torture me with lies.
While I got drunk, you lit my darkened lawn
With nets of light, and set her there, to gaze
In rapture at you captured in my garden.

Why don't you gloat less brightly? Set T.V.
Full in the forehead of your jealous mind?
Sit her on my sofa drinking wine with me
While I admire her in my drunken kind?

No mercy, moon, I see, you choose to shine
Making a monkey of my rival face:
She is so free french windows cannot hold her

As on her face, as on her fragrant shoulder,
You drop your balm, your soul-enchanting lies,
And steal from me what heaven knows is mine.

VI

Behold the dark, alone, with nothing in it,
Except despair, your poverty, and death.
Then, like a switch within, electric light
Broadcast through the bedroom where you breathe.

This is my state. I'm richer than the wild
And idle rich burning the bloom of youth,
For love alone is money, and the gold
The rich transcend the struggle to this truth.

Quicker than blinkers, love decides the price
Of oxygen and hydrogen no less
By which we breathe and eat or come to grace

Glowing in the knowledge of each other.
Ah yes, it's true, the love without the lover
Is like the bowl without the grains of rice.

Sebastian Barker

Love And His Lexis

Jane Harris

It is autumn, evening in Amadora. A posse of gypsies struts along the railway track; nearby in the shopping centre washroom, the attendant moans about vanishing toilet rolls, while a magician pockets her tips; upstairs in the language school, the director snorts himself awake, blinks at the fluorescence above his desk and resolves aloud to make this definitely, absolutely, his final season in goal for the English soccer team. There is modest applause and some wolf-whistling from his Upper Intermediate class.

English! International language! Language of wealth! American movie and computer manual! The door-opener! Yet Carlos Constantinho found he was the only student on the Elementary course. How excruciating. Or so he thought until he saw his teacher.

"Ahem," said Kate, looking at the floor. "Don't worry, more students start next week."

But no-one else ever did enrol in Elementary and, secretly, Carlos was glad. Glad because of Kate. Oh Kate! She wasn't beautiful but she exuded something, something he couldn't put into words. He imagined she might have stumbled out of a tangle of warm sheets straight into the classroom and he wondered what it would be like to unbutton and peel back her cardigan.

He began to take particular care in dressing in anticipation of his evening lesson. He had a spectacular collection of sweaters so that as he shrugged off his jacket, Kate would say: "Oh Carlos, another lovely sweater!"

These English sounds unleashed in him a squirm of pleasure, the intensity of which threatened to manifest itself physically. He perfected a move into his chair to camouflage his embarrassment: a pirouette tinged with worldly-weariness; a mid-point twist of his legs each around the other then, just as he arsed the seat, the thrust of his torso at an angle. Johnny on the spot; a corkscrew of attentiveness. Pristine in cashmere, tucked into primary colours like an elegant, impudent sweet, he adored her.

Kate sat beside him to correct his exercises, loose hair screening her face. She had a way of hooking one foot behind the tubular metal of the chair and balancing her other ankle on the flat of her thigh, in semi-lotus. How intimate the denim-clad leg with his own. How vaguely grubby the denim.

"Nice work Carlos" was all she ever said, as her hand moved across the pages in his jotter. Each time she reached out to write on the board, his eyes fastened on a hole in her cardigan just underneath the shoulder. What would happen if he slid his finger inside and stroked the musk that laced the secret place below her arm?

Once, she borrowed his pen and her fingernail dragged accidentally along his palm. Carlos felt as if he'd grasped a shorting wire. The shock penetrated his heart; his diaphragm vibrated electric blue and, somewhere, lightning licked the surface of a prism-shaped crystal. He became aware of a happy ache lurking behind the book in his lap and considered flicking it across the room with one neat thrust of his pelvic muscles.

Eroticism like this made concentration elusive during the day. Slumped at his desk or computer terminal, his thoughts took on the repetitive qualities of a rather seedy slide-show:

In a sealed capsule in the furthest reaches of the solar system, he rests his head and nuzzles the swellings in the front of Kate's cardigan. He can observe the activities of the earthlings far below, hear their voices pulse in aural stroboscope. Kate is caressing the little hairs on the back of his neck and counting her buttons: three, four, five. Carlos lifts his head to help her count: six, seven, eight, but is always shaken from the most interesting part of the dream by a terrestrial, waving sheets of paper at him, demanding calculations, his attention, an answer.

Numbers and figures zoomed into and out of focus beneath his nose, but Kate was somewhere safe in the back of his mind and the capsule was snug and rations could be eked out until splashdown.

His muscles tightened and relaxed, counting down to the moment when they could propel him from his building and across the park to the language school. If he was early, which he contrived to be most of the time, and she was available, which he suspected *she* engineered, they'd run downstairs to the cafe where she'd drink coffee and talk and he'd drink nothing and listen.

She told him stories about Ireland, a mystical land he associated with golf, and a bewildering assortment of military initials. He made general sense of what she said by homing in on the emotions in her voice; the rest he traced together with love and his lexis. Bubbles of words streamed past, tickling him. Beautiful, thought Carlos. She was 28, she said. He wondered why she'd never married: 28 was quite old, still to be single.

In the classroom, whenever they reached a phrase of particular importance, she'd hold up her left hand and transform each finger on it into a word, highlighting the separate components of the sentence.

I/LOVE/YOU/KATE. That would be four fingers, Carlos calculated.

/I/ on the little finger /love/ on the ring finger /you/ on the middle finger and /Kate/ on the index.

I LOVE YOU KATE. Repeat? I love you sweet Kate.

Now where's the emphasis in that sentence, Kate?

He bought her a rose for her birthday. He knew the date because she'd used it as an example for Section Three in the course-book: YEAR AND AGE, and he'd made a careful note of it after class. The rose was wrapped in cellophane and waxy scarlet ribbons. Four green tendrils attached to the top of the stem; nine visible cochineal petals folded around the heart. It looked almost edible, moulded from a rich almond paste.

He sneaked up on Kate as she rearranged chairs in the room and yanked the flower from behind his back, grinning, like a cheerful gunfighter. Kate flinched. "Carlos! How lovely. Thank you!"

He searched her face for messages. Tears, certainly. Her mouth twitching. The forehead puckered in confusion, darkened into misery. A feeble smile. Then she sprayed a salvo of English at him. He pounced on a single reassuring word, "Water" (Section Four: AT THE CAFE; "A glass of water please.") just as, on his first day at infant school, he'd sought out the scarlet of his mother's lips in the crowds outside. But before he could decipher what Kate meant, she'd already hurried out of the classroom.

Carlos doodled in the margin of his notebook. His teacher returned just as he was adding the final touches to an astronaut's helmet. She was clutching the flower in a lemonade bottle and he noticed a charcoal smudge of mascara on the puff of skin beneath her right eyelid.

"Thank you Carlos," she said, launching straight into Section Seven: (FORMAL APOLOGIES; "I'm terribly sorry." "It doesn't matter.")

"Excuse me Kate, but…"

She raised her left eyebrow at him.

"There is black, here," said Carlos, touching his own face, giving Kate a mirror image. He wanted to cradle her cheek and smooth away the tear-stain with his thumb. And didn't.

It is five to six. In a building opposite the park in a bright classroom a woman in a cardigan wipes the whiteboard and sits down next to a solitary student. It is the last lesson of term. Her hair is blonde. She smiles and places a slim box on the arm of her student's chair. Click. A cassette. It has been wrapped in blue paper and yellow ribbons. The student's cheeks flush. Perhaps the teacher is 30 centimetres away from him: the length of his ruler.

He is reaching for his jacket, for her present, just as she leans forward and kisses him on both cheeks. Her hair tickles his nose twice and for a second he considers forgetting custom and snuggling his face into it, smothering himself in her scent. But he is too late.

The woman sits back, staring – as if trying to decide something – at his mouth. She does this for what seems a very long time. At length, she sighs. She looks tired, her sigh is brief and hopeless. Hesitantly she lifts her hand, kisses her middle finger — YOU — and lays it on her student's mouth. His eyes close. If he opens them he will explode. The finger is warm. It rests on his lower lip and he wonders if he should suck it. He listens, hearing blood pulsing in his ears and two people trying hard to breathe normally. He contemplates nibbling, biting, making a joke, but dismisses these as foolish and is just about to relax his lips and let the finger slide between his teeth when the faint pressure on his mouth is gone and the classroom door is open.

It is only as he sits down on the train that he realises he has forgotten to give her the present.

Over Christmas, Carlos visited his father by the sea. Scuffing along the beach, his shoes full of sand, his head full of Kate, he attempted to picture what she was doing. Right at that moment, perhaps as he lobbed a pine-cone into the sticky black surf. Splish. Maybe she was thinking of him. Sploosh. Maybe she had a boyfriend. She never mentioned one. No, impossible then. Could he invite her out here for the weekend? Hadn't he heard somewhere that students and teachers shouldn't socialise? Splash!

He practised the words of his invitation as he waited in class for Kate at the beginning of the second term: "Hello Kate. Do you like to come to Apple Beach? Kate, maybe better, Hi!; Hi! I go to Apple Beach, you want to come with? Hello…"

"Hello Carlos," said the woman closing the classroom door. "I'm Jill your new teacher."

Carlos looked at the woman and the pen he was holding broke. He struggled for breath and politeness. "But where is Kate please?"

A thin string of beads emphasised the thickness of the woman's neck; her blouse was shiny and had straight creases ironed into the arms.

"Ah Kate." She pulled air through her teeth, as if she was in pain. "Kate went back to England. Not well. Do you understand, ill?" The woman mimed someone vomiting.

"Yes, yes, I understand" Carlos said hastily, though he didn't. Kate came from Ireland, not England. Kate was never sick. He wanted to grab the woman's beads and choke her.

"Anyway I'm from England too and we'll get along fine. So, what's your surname, hmmm?"

"Constantinho." The constant, the loyal, the faithful. What then did that make Kate? For she'd left him.

"Con-stan-tee-no. And how old are you Carlos Constantinho?"

It didn't seem possible. Hundreds, thousands of kilometres away. Across oceans. And now he could never ask her to the beach house. No gathering of pine-cones hand in hand. She could have laid her finger on his mouth again, and then, the kiss: tongue touching tongue as the waves lapped and sucked at the shore.

"Carlos. How old are you, hmmm?"

"Oh. I'm sorry; 13. I'm 13 years old." (Section Three: YEAR AND AGE. "How old are you?" "I'm 28; How old are you?" "I'm 13.")

"Good," mooed the woman. "Open your book at page 46, like a good boy. No, 46, that's it. Now, Carlos, what can you see in the picture, hmmm?"

An oily fog of chestnut smoke scuds towards the park. It is dusk. The town hall spells out a New Year greeting in lightbulbs: *Prospero Ano Novo.* From the shopping centre, digital tunes piddle and evaporate into the contained hysteria of shoppers, the soggy rubbish and the impatient traffic. Luis, King of Chestnuts, chews gum. He waits a long time for a customer.

Jane Harris

AN AULD SANG DIRLS AGAIN

THE CEILIDH HOUSE

The High Street wis yince a hub o music, poetry an' talk.
The Ceilidh House pits back that tradeetioun.

Folk nichts – poetry nichts – an aye-bidan come-aa-ye

Ilka nicht o the week a new stramash!

Cleik yer pals in fur a pint or a dram. Ye'll hae a waarm walcome.

Eldritch neuks and crannies fur smaa foregaitherings
Cellar haa fur middlin-scale occasiouns

The Ceilidh House, 9 Hunter Square, Edinburgh EH1 1QW
Heid Wanger: Cy Laurie
Tel 031-220 1550

Graham Fulton

Cream of Scottish Youth

rolled

trousers to knees and
danced a weird waltz.

Chucked bangers at club-feet,
snow at girls' faces,
crisp bags full of frogspawn slop.

Sat among rocks, wore Harlequin socks,
rabbit ear collars and baratheas, spat
on the heads of waggy yap dogs
allowed to run free by owners.
Rolled

jumper sleeves to elbows
and pretended to be Thalidomide.
Smoked
singles
bought from ice cream vans,
scuffed mushy leaves with best shoes, kicked
puddle-twigs at the dumb sun as the wind
swiped through big branches, scurried
among big shadows.
Tumbled,

yelling, from dizzy swish roundabouts,
pelted the swans in the dam with cans,
tore the pages from the brainyboy's books
then tipped his schoolbag upside down,
lit fires just for the hell of it, splashed
scruffy steam gold against the oaks

that had seen it all before.

Ate banana and marmite rolls
as gloom curdled in the cloakroom.
Looked at photos of whopper breasts,
studied photos of open legs,
fell over each other to sniff

the future.
Fumbled
in panties at puberty parties,
swallowed Pale Ale, Newcastle Brown,
Breaker Malt Liquor and Eldorado.
Gathered at night to sit on walls
or topple sun-dials onto grass.
Made scratchy marks on sheds and lamp-posts,
squirted stinking, chemist perfumes
onto clothes of teeth-brace boys,
spluttered over thick Panatellas,
chewed on borrowed plastic pipes.
Dropped lit matches into postboxes,
said the words "fanny", "gobble" and "spunk",
spooned in shagalley toothpaste dark,
fell over each other to reach

the sex.
Grew
hair long, got it chopped off,
did everything wrong, everything
right.
Threw slushballs at respectable windows,
stones at clocks, rocks at stars
and cruised cobbled wynds with springs
in heels,
skated, laughing, into the void, fell over
each other to ask

the time.
Rolled

Trousers to knees and
danced a daft can-can.
Rolled back to ankles, hobbled
for home, the whipped

cream of Scotland's dream.

Kirk Douglas Lookalikes Have Some Fun

The Kirk Douglas lookalike
                            wears a hat,
a polo neck sweater,
                            sensible socks.
He plays the wireless,
                            drinks hot milk,
fingers pin-ups
                     of filmstar girls.
His world revolves
                    around fur.
Dimples
        Vikings
               Rugged teeth.

The ship slices
                   through Arctic ice.
He leaps
          from the rope
when they reach
                the seals,
shuffle-skids
                 to the nearest mother.
She makes a noise
                 to scare him off.
He brings his club
                 down on her skull.
A stunning display
               of skill.
A dull
        perfect crunch.

He sticks a spike
                 into her pup,
pulls it by
           the splashed handle
with the spike
               lodged in its brain.
The pup is thrown
                 on a pile of pups,

lies blinking
        into sun,
a red trench
        in its face.
Someone sees it
        still alive,
pokes a spike
        three more times.
An awesome display
        of strength.
A sharp
        lunatic wind.

The Norwegian sealer
        wears trousers
held up with a belt.
        He plays cards,
collects his bonus,
        cleans his hands
with carbolic soap.
        It is
a standard
        hygiene routine.
His world bobs
        on a flood
of blood.

Cameras
        Action
        Thrills and spills.
He blows cold kisses
        to his wife
who makes a noise
        to welcome him home.
She is pretty
        with blonde hair,
his children are cute
        with big round eyes.
They sleep in pink beds
        on sheets
as soft
        as smashed-in
        heads.

The Seamstress and the Sculptor

She makes costumes
for fairy-tales. He stays,
most days,
in bed.

She wears a short skirt, keeps tugging it
down, slipping
uncomfortably into her role, trying
to make him want her
again.
Plopping coins in wishing wells,
painting nails, casting spells.

At a party
three weeks before Halloween
she strokes the thighs of strangers.
He explains
to the riveted throng
how his chosen career has lost its charm
and how
now any old job will do.
Butcher, baker, robotmaker.
Machinery carving into his eyes, stripping
the features from his face.

Treading water forever
in a hand-me-down town
full of dried-up clay.

He spews
jokes,
but his head is packed
with the long ride home in a dark hackney,
fare-light
clicking relentlessly on.

She dreams of the kiss
that will wake
him up,
pours clumsy nothings into his ear.
Drowns in the desert
of bedspace between them each night.

Magnificent Achievements of Mankind

Water pistols and
rolls of caps. skeleton families
herded on trains,
creative pain tested
on pigs, electrodes
stuck to genitals
in the dressing rooms
of football stadiums. smooth

submarines full of Polaris,
bows and arrows, Anthrax warheads,
catapults, muskets, blades, grenades
on and on, on
and on
and cluster neutron phosphorous bombs, boys
with cocky sepia grins
slipping of duckboards
sinking down into
fossilpulp bloodbone horsecorpse mud
with bullet-drilled skulls and rag doll wire
gurgling and blind on a madhouse cot
as doctors scribble, generals nod
and bugles show
the way
ahead to
nothing left but shadows and smoke, a lovely
light as the world bursts. and rectums

jabbed with broken glass, skeleton families
showered with gas,
bazookas grapeshot sticks and stones,
piano wire men dancing on hooks.
and sharp uniformed genocide experts
clubbing women to the ground
and mutant stillbirths in jars on shelves
children screaming on dirt roads with
their napalm jelly flesh on fire.

Graham Fulton

Neil M Gunn – A New Awakening

Dairmid Gunn

In an article to mark the Neil Gunn centenary year, J B Pick wrote "When Neil Gunn died in 1973, he was out of fashion and out of print. He hadn't published a book since 1956, and then it was the oddly elusive spiritual autobiography, *the Atom of Delight*, which was little-understood and didn't sell." Now in 1992, one year after the centenary, all his major works are in print, an impressive total of 20 novels. Why such a change in fortune? I want to address this resurgence of interest in Gunn and his work, the current popularity of his novels, the books written about the man and his *oeuvre*, and the critics' response.

The importance of the centenary of his birth I can only term a new awakening; but even in the early 1970s interest in Gunn's work was not dead – it had simply reached a low ebb. By the mid-70s, *The Silver Darlings* (Faber), *Highland River* (Arrow Books) and a clutch of books including *Young Art and Old Hector, The Green Isle of the Great Deep, Morning Tide* and *Butcher's Broom* – all Souvenir Press in London – were in print. Perhaps the resurgence in the 1970s of interest in things Scottish, combined with the improving fortunes of the SNP, helped to act as a catalyst to a renewal of enthusiasm for Gunn's work. But there was more to it than that, and in that context I should like to pick up John Pick's description of *The Atom of Delight* as being oddly elusive. Gunn's books may have been set in Scotland but they all contained intimations of life at several levels.

In his writings there was something for everyone – even in the restless decades of the '70s and '80s. For the thoughtful, there was philosophy; for the rootless, roots; for pessimists, optimism; and for the general reader usually a good story enhanced by the author's genius for conveying the spirit of Scotland both in human and animistic terms. His novels catered for the mood of the discerning reader. If a reader wishes melodrama, there is *The Lost Glen*, an angry young man's book; if a dialogue between youth and old age, *Young Art and Old Master*; if a Brave New World, *The Green Isle of the Great Deep*; if a search for personal wholeness, *Highland River* and *The Atom of Delight*; if a coming to terms with life, *Blood Hunt* and *The Silver Bough*. Douglas Gifford argues, and I think rightly, that *The Silver Darlings*, that saga of the boom years in the herring industry, is the finest balance of metaphysical speculation and concrete epic-making that any fiction writer in English has achieved this century. Gunn never writes the same book twice. The stories change although the levels within them remain.

Yet the accusation frequently pops up from the pen of a critic that Gunn is too elusive, a mystic who has lost touch with reality. Recently, Richard Drew, now with Chambers, persuaded me to allow *Off in a Boat* to be republished. This marvellous odyssey in the seas around the Hebrides is more than a travelogue spiced with philosophy – a perfect example of how to break with routine, sell up and start a new life. We frequently moan: "if only I could have peace and quiet to do all the things I want to do" – Gunn had the courage of his convictions to break with routine. But his feet are again firmly on the ground in a book that has been called a spiritual survey, *Whisky and Scotland* . It is an anchor work for whisky enthusiasts and a classic of its sort. He had the same regard for the great Scottish drink as the French connoisseur has for a *grand vin*.

Although not a politician by nature, Gunn felt deeply enough about Scotland to participate in the founding of what is now the Scottish National Party. In the 1930s his house in Inverness saw many a meeting of those who believed that Scotland should have more say in its destiny. As always he was positive – not anti-English or anti-anything; simply pro-Scots and pro the contribution a small community could make to mankind. This deep-rooted passion for his country and the small nation so clearly expressed in his essay "Nationalism and Internationalism" (published in *Landscape and Light* and *The Man Who Came Back*) and implicit in so many of his novels is ample proof that Gunn was very much in touch with everyday problems.

The intrinsic merit of his writing and his concern for the here and now, however, do not fully explain his current popularity. There have been other major contributory factors. They range from the Scottish Arts Council Neil Gunn Fellowship, a fellowship that includes in its membership such illustrious foreign authors as Heinrich Böll, Saul Bellow, Ruth Jabvala, Mario Llosa and Nadine Gardiner, to the significant number of books written by those who have been fascinated by one aspect or another of the writer's life and work. More immediately, of course, there have been the celebrations all over Scotland to mark the centenary of Neil Gunn's birth.

Although the establishing of the Neil Gunn Fellowship, a fact known to the author before his death and an idea that gave him great pleasure, heralded greater recognition of his works and a claim for international status, that in itself would not have been enough to engender a continuing revival. The much-needed biography came in 1981 in the authoritative and sensitive *A Highland Life* (John Murray; later Polygon), by critic and novelist J B Pick and the American specialist in Scottish literature, Francis Hart. A winner of the SAC Book Award, it was quickly acclaimed as a triumph – a revealing insight into a person as complex as Proust. His biographers knew and liked Gunn, but often had to "interpret" him through his works. This book drew the attention of the reading public again to Gunn's works, even the most obscure.

In the 1980s there followed a series of critical works. Douglas Gifford's *Gunn and Gibbon*; *Landscape and Light* (AUP) ed Alistair McCleery, a collection of Gunn's essays; *The Novels of Neil M Gunn, A Critical Study* by Margery McCulloch (Scottish Academic Press) covers all Gunn's novels;

A Celebration of the Light (Canongate, 1987) by John Burns dwells on Neil Gunn's interest in Buddhism and Taoism so apparent in the spiritual auto-biography *The Atom of Delight*. C J L Stokoe's *A Bibliography of the Works of Neil M Gunn* (AUP, 1987) is a valuable contribution to Gunn scholarship. J B Pick's *Neil M Gunn – Selected Letters* (Polygon, 1988) covers Gunn's development as a writer and also the post-writing period when he had still so much to contribute to cultural life. The impact made by these books was bolstered by a BBC film of *Blood Hunt*, adapted by Stewart Conn.

When 1991, the Centenary Year was reached, nearly all Gunn's major works were in print and interest in them was at a satisfactorily high level. But more books were to come in that year of celebration. *A Writers' Ceilidh for Neil Gunn* (Balnain Books, 1991) is a tribute in the form of creative work from a collection of talented Scottish writers and poets. *Neil Gunn's Country* (Chambers, 1991) Edited by Isobel Murray and myself, is a collection of essays on the author by members of the dwindling band of those who knew him. *The Fabulous Matter of Fact* (EUP, 1991) is a comprehensive study by Richard Price of all Gunn's novels, including an early unpublished novel *The Poaching at Grianan*. *The Man Who Came Back* edited by Margery McCulloch contains a carefully-chosen selection of short stories and essays, with a title that is pregnant with meaning.

Against this background of interest more novels were republished. *Highland River* (Canongate) made its reappearance; *Wild Geese Overhead* (Chambers), an early novel set in Glasgow, was also republished to join the series started by Richard Drew and continued by Chambers, which includes such novels as *The Lost Chart*, *The Lost Glen*, *The other Landscape*, *Second Sight* and *Off in a Boat*. Souvenir Press, clinging to its grouping of some of Gunn's best novels, came out with new editions of *Butcher's Broom* and *The Green Isle of the Great Deep*.

All this activity on the Neil Gunn front seems to indicate that all that can be done has been done to portray the author through his works. Two books, however, await republishing. His first novel, *The Poaching at Grianan*, and the collection of short stories entitled *Hidden Doors*. The first falls far short of his other novels in depth, style and structure; it is an interesting period piece and is perhaps comparable to some of the books written by his Irish friend and contemporary, Maurice Walsh. Some of the stories from *Hidden Doors* stray into another and more refined and sophisticated collection, *The White Hour*, now republished by Richard Drew/Chambers. *Hidden Doors* has much to commend it and, almost certainly, will be republished.

Interest in further research remains and it is not confined to Scotland. Certain of Gunn's books have been published in German and Spanish; indeed the great Jung himself was fascinated by the anti-Utopian *Green Isle of the Great Deep*. Some time ago Jung's grandson, also a psychoanalyst, opened negotiations with me over the possibility of republishing *The Green Isle* in German. Continental interest in this extraordinary book is not confined to Germany: Lyon University Press is in the process of publishing a first French version. On the subject of France, one of the most interesting dissertations I have read on Gunn recently was written by Philippe Laplace, studying at Brest University for his Doctorate. The title he chose was *La Recherche de L'Identité dans les romans de Neil Gunn*.

The appearance of new books may have been the clearest manifestation of interest in the writer and his work in his Centenary Year; there were, of course, others. At the Edinburgh Book Festival last summer a successful International Writers' Conference was held on aspects of the novel. At the Festival itself there were celebrations of Neil Gunn's life and work: Marjory McNeil and Mike Moran can only be congratulated on their interpretation of the man and his work. Earlier a travelling exhibition on Gunn, mounted by the National Library of Scotland, had begun its tour of the Lowlands and Highlands. This exhibition was launched at a conference on Gunn, organised by Alan Spence, writer in residence at Edinburgh University. Later in the year, the Eden Court production of Aonghas Macneacail's *Atoms of Delight*, skilfully mixing Gunn's experiences and philosophy with unforgettable episodes from the novels, toured to Highland locations close to the author's heart, memorably in Dunbeath on 8 November 1991, the centenary itself, when I unveiled a commemorative statue in Dunbeath harbour. The aurora borealis that night saluted the occasion with a spectacular display.

What was particularly pleasing, and what would have delighted Gunn himself, were the activities of groups of devotees living in the two areas that had meant so much to him – Dingwall and its hinterland, and Caithness. The Ross & Cromarty District Council and the Neil Gunn Memorial Trust have kept his name to the fore in the area in which he enjoyed his most fruitful years. The Neil Gunn Society, based in Caithness, has done the same thing further north. Tourists north of Inverness are now made fully aware of the existence of this great Scottish writer, while the local people now realise the stature of this man who had spent most of his life in the north.

Whether or not my theory of why Gunn is still popular with readers 19 years after his death and 36 years after his last major work, *The Atom of Delight*, is correct is of little consequence. There could be other explanations and I cannot resist quoting Richard Drew when he said he could market Neil Gunn's books even if they were wrapped up in brown paper. The fact remains that he is still popular among readers, young and old. In the output of a writer who has written so much, there must be variations in the standards of his works and also variations in the degree of appreciation on the part of his readers. His philosophical bent of mind has clearly caused some critics considerable concern. There are accusations of his using his mysticism as a sort of smoke screen to conceal a woolliness of thought; there are claims that he distorted history and was "sexist" in some of his writings.

I have always felt that in some Lowland minds there is a deep distrust of the Highland imagination. Jokes are made by Lowlanders about the northern communities in the same way as the English make them about the Irish. If Gunn was saddened by some of the criticism levelled at him, he was rarely embittered. He saw the negative and destructive criticism as a failure on his part to convey to others what was profound and life-enhancing. The word "mystic" for him meant someone who had a clarity of vision, generally associated with the great Eastern philosophers whom he so greatly admired. His view of history centred round the concept that it was people who were the warp and woof of civilisation as it moved forwards with noticeable or historical events. In his view, it was the womenfolk within communities which held them together and provided an element of continuity. Some critics react to this positioning of women in the heart of things, thinking that somehow or other the author is 'putting them in their place'. Perhaps they do not appreciate that Gunn is according women a very important place in the scheme of things. In the small fishing village in which he lived men and women had distinct spheres of interest. The sea was the man's preserve; the land the women's. Each was equally important. This was a reflexion of a community at certain moments of time. I accept that such a division is more difficult to apply to an urban society where men and women are often occupied with the same tasks and where the home is not always the woman's preserve. In his essay in *Neil Gunn's Country* when discussing *Highland River* and *The Serpent*, Professor Hart touches on Gunn's changing intuition of women and finds a key in the latter novel when he writes:

> Tom [the central character] is led to this revelation by his reading, by his discovery of Rousseau of "the feminine mind", as opposed to the male categories, the philosophical absolutes, the masculine rules of life.

In *Blood Hunt* Hart claims that in Sandy, the central character, there is a male character who has effectively assumed the traditional role of the woman – the housekeeper, the practical caretaker, the instinctive protector against male categories of law and justice. Sandy is both paternal and maternal. And that could work in the case of a female version of Sandy.

A final criticism that has been levelled at Gunn is self-infatuation, an immense egoism. I find this accusation quite extraordinary. The critic had obviously not understood *The Atom of Delight* and Gunn's preoccupation in the book of ridding himself of "self". Anyway, there is nothing wrong with a good dose of introspection. It would be fitting to end this article with a free translation of a verse from one of Russia's greatest poets, Tyutchev, who, in his poem "Silentium", argues for a certain amount of introspection and secrecy.

> Be silent, hide yourself, and conceal your feelings and your dreams.

> Let them rise and set in the depth of your soul, silently, like stars in the night; contemplate them with admiration, and be silent.

Gunn certainly listened, but perhaps was more in tune with the writer of the Book of Ecclesiastes, who was also on a quest for wisdom: "To everything there is a season, and a time to every purpose under the heaven … a time to keep silence, and a time to speak."   **Dairmid Gunn**

TS Eliot in Inverness, 1935, during a visit to Gunn
(National Library of Scotland)

Neil Gunn and the Criticism of T S Eliot

Richard Price

> What we can do is to use our minds, remembering that a tradition without intelligence is not worth having, to discover what is the best life for us not as a political abstraction, but as a particular people in a particular place; what in the past is worth preserving and what should be rejected; and what conditions, within our power to bring about, would foster the society that we desire.
>
> **T S Eliot,** *After Strange Gods*

Neil Gunn met T S Eliot at least three times in his life: in 1933, 1935 and 1937. That these encounters took place far from the poet's London workplace – at the Gunn home in Inverness – might be expected to raise an eyebrow or two among Eliot scholars. Yet each of Eliot's biographers, when mentioning his visit to the Highlands, neglects to name Gunn. Eliot's 1933 trip, several hundred miles by car from Glasgow to Inverness in *November*, is described as if it had no more consequence than a summer evening jaunt.

Some writers on the Scottish Rennaisance, have been quicker to mark the significance of Eliot's visits. Hart and Pick in their biography of Gunn explain the later visits in terms of Eliot's position as a director of Faber, of which Gunn's publisher, Porpoise Press, was by then an agency. On the 1935 visit Eliot was accompanied by Frank Morley (also from Faber) and Alfred Harcourt (from Harcourt Brace, Eliot's American publisher.

Between the 1935 and 1937 visit *Highland River* (1937) was written and published. The latter encounter between Eliot and Gunn can be seen again in publishing terms, a consolidatory visit, an attempt by Faber to show special interest in an author promising even bigger things. *Highland River* was enough of a commercial success to persuade Gunn to take up writing as a full-time occupation (its critical success was recognised in 1938 when it won the James Tait Black Memorial Prize). This release from the Civil Service enabled him, while writing other novels, short stories, and essays, to research and complete his magnum opus *The Silver Darlings* (1941).

When we look at the first visit, one not covered by Hart and Pick, the publisher connection suggests itself, too. Eliot was accompanied by Harcourt's partner, Donald Brace, by Morley, and also by the novelist George Blake, a director both of Porpoise and Faber. Brace read and commented on *Butcher's Broom* in 1934 and Harcourt Brace published it in 1935 – further indication of the close attention Gunn's publishers paid him.

Eliot and the Scottish Renaissance

Eliot's friend Morley, in a letter to Blake, praised the *The Lost Glen* as a noble failure, remarking on its ambition but also on its inability to make symbolic episodes say enough. He compared it to *Hamlet* in a deliberately analagous way to Eliot's 1919 study of the play. Though he admired Gunn's concentration – "The wealth of attention he's given to this problem wd be inconceivable to an ordinary bastard," Morley felt Gunn had failed to rise to the enormity of his theme. Because he felt keenly the parallels between the Highlands and his native Southern states of America, he expected better: "If Gunn does anything unworthy of his theme by God I'll lynch him."

Morley's identification with Gunn is unlikely to have been missed by an Eliot already sensitive to the aspirations of the Scottish Renaissance. Eliot had been in correspondence with MacDiarmid since 1930. He accepted his essay 'English Ascendancy in British Literature' for *The Criterion* in 1931, and the poem 'Second Hymn to Lenin' for the same journal in 1932. Correspondence between the two poets seems to have thinned, however, by mid-1932, though it resumes towards the end of the 1930s. This 'fallow' period in their long-distance relationship was exactly when Eliot was in much closer contact with Gunn.

Robert Crawford has highlighted Eliot's only Scottish poem, 'Rannoch, by Glencoe' as "a piece of political analysis, based partly, perhaps, on Eliot's own meetings and contacts with Scottish writers including Gunn, Muir – and MacDiarmid". That it was after his first visit to the Gunns when Eliot stopped to see Rannoch Moor confirms Crawford's assertion that Eliot was responding to Scottish politics. The poem shares the bitterness and the locale one finds in early Gunn: a frustration with a Highlands in decay, with a nation skilled only in self-defeat. Like all Gunn's novels before *Highland River*, it is concerned with Scotland's apparent failure to rise above the tragedies of its history – "Pride snapped,/ Shadow of pride is long, in the long pass/ No concurrence of bone." Scotland had become, as *The Lost Glen* and *Butcher's Broom* showed, a semi-colonial country. It was implicated in the rise of the British Empire but was also a victim of it. Scotland was where "the patient stag/ Breeds for the rifle."

Following Eliot's visit, Gunn wrote to MacDiarmid in terms that suggest that poet and novelist had discussed nationalism and literature at length:

> ... We were talking about you the other night when a car load of tough guys, including T. S. Eliot, descended upon us. I didn't get to bed until 5 a.m. Reminded me of some nights you and I used to have in the old days! No chance of you coming this way? If at all possible, make a night of it. The whole Scottish situation requires review.

The comparison of Eliot to a latter-day MacDiarmid is a telling one. In the 1920s MacDiarmid encouraged Gunn to consider himself as a novelist of national importance. The letter also conveys Gunn's sense of urgency: "The whole Scottish situation requires review."

Gunn had been working during 1933 for the National Party of Scotland in an attempt to iron out differences between the National Party and the Scottish Party. The danger of splitting the small but growing nationalist vote was avoided when negotiations between the two parties culminated , a month after Eliot's visit, in the establishment of the Scottish National Party.

Eliot had arrived at Gunn's door when the novelist was at the height of his nationalist political involvement.

After Strange Gods

Eliot's responsiveness to nationalist thinking surfaces in *After Strange Gods: a Primer of Modern Heresy* (London: Faber, 1934), a collection of three lectures delivered at the University of Virginia in April 1933. This book shows that Eliot early on was explicitly making the connection between the political views of the Renaissance writers and those writers of the Southern states who were known as 'the Agrarians'. The Agrarian Movement, including such writers as Allen Tate and John Crowe Ransome, opposed the condescension of the northern victors of the American Civil War, championing the different traditions of the South and criticising the allegiance of advances in technology with centralised control of the masses. The issue Eliot discusses here place Gunn and the Scottish Renaissance within the context of Western literature as a whole. Eliot argued, for example, that crossing from a Northern state into a Southern state "is as definite an experience as to cross from England to Wales, almost as definite as to cross the English Channel. And the differences here, with no difference of language or race to support them, have had to survive the immense pressure towards monotony exerted by the industrial expansion of the latter part of the nineteenth century and the first part of the twentieth century.".

That emphasis on "language and race" being *not necessarily relevant* to the issue of nationality is crucial to the debates occuring within the Renaissance. Much earlier, in 1928, Gunn focused on Eliot's suggestion in his 'Introduction to the Method of Paul Valéry', that discussion of Yeats as a poet had to admit his Irishness, and the way Irish poets used the English language. From this, Gunn argued, it followed that the Scottish writer choosing to use English as the medium of communication should be aware of his predecessors *within the Scottish tradition* and, given that self-awareness, "his English will *slowly* find its own significant pattern, as Irishman or American has found his pattern". Gunn's change from his most densely distributed use of Scots in *The Grey Coast* (1926) to an English with a Scottish inflection in all the other novels after it illustrates this principle.

Eliot's identification of industrialisation as antithetic to cultural distinctiveness is apposite to Gunn's *oeuvre*, too. In his novels, city, especially the Scottish city, is usually treated in terms of promise mismanaged and unfulfilled. *The Green Isle of the Great Deep* is concerned with what happens to the individual when the work process is systemized for "economic" reasons. Here is the whole question of control of peripheries by city bureaucracies, a political model that has clear relevance to Gunn's nationalism. In *After Strange Gods*, Eliot described how such a suspicion of "centres" was only to be expected:

> When [the nation] becomes no more than a centralised machinery it may affect some of its parts to their detriment, or to what they believe to be their detriment; and we get the regional movements which have appeared within recent years. It is only a law of nature, that local patriotism, when it represents a distinct tradition and culture, takes precedence over a more abstract national patriotism.

Eliot seems here to be thinking in terms of "regions" and "local patriotism" rather than countries-within-countries, but a footnote shows he has been directly influenced by Scottish nationalism.

> I have in mind Mr Chesterton and his 'Distribution', Mr Christopher Dawson (*The Making of Europe*) ... the views of Mr Allen Tate ...in *I'll Take my Stand*, and those of several Scottish nationalists.

This indicates how the ideas that the Renaissance had been generating were apposite to Eliot's notions of spiritual alternatives to centralist decadence.

Gunn had made the connection between the American south and Scottish nationalism in *The Lost Glen* (published as a book in 1932 but serialised in *The Scots Magazine* in 1928). This occurs in the book at a concert for the benefit of the new American laird. Gunn introduces the rich landowner's son – whose party-piece is to sing the Southern rallying call, 'Dixie'. It is a moment of dark irony, an irony reinforced by what follows the sham concert: an energetic and erotic ceilidh organised by and for the villagers themselves.

The phrase "after strange gods" appears in *Sun Circle*, published in May 1933, well before Gunn could have read Eliot's lectures. Eliot may have picked the phrase up from Gunn: the lectures were not brought together under their common title until their publication in 1934. The phrase occurs in *Sun Circle* when the narrator is discussing a throwback to human sacrifice in the face of desperation at the recent defeat of the Celts before the Vikings. During a transitional period between a pagan polytheism and the rise of the Celtic Church:

> ...seeking after strange gods. That god of the Christian, for example; who is a white pale god, pleasant in the sun, but for such an hour as this of what power, of what value? a puny crying god, who was himself sac- rificed. No power in him, no fierceness; no storm set in black brows, no wind-threshing vengeance, no terror; no sacrifices to be made to him, no appeasement, no dark drink. What did he know of the flesh and the vitals?

Faced with the apparent failure of Christianity to defend them, the Celts revert to older practices. Breeta, the book's heroine, is seized for sacrifice. She is saved only by a fire, instigated by the Vikings, that burns down the Celts' place of pagan worship. Though "after strange gods" sounds familiar, this precise combination of words does not occur in the Bible. There is, however, an echo: "If ye forsake the Lord and serve strange gods, then he will turn and do you hurt, and consume you, after that he hath done you good." (Joshua, 24:20). The allusion is actually in ironic contra-distinction to the narrator's view of the Christian god as feeble. Gunn, who has drawn a sympathetic portrait of early Christianity in the book, is turning the allusion around: *the Christian God* is the strange but meek god, and the earlier gods familiar but savage. The novel is a progression away from the bloodthirsty aspects of preChristian religion towards at least the hope of some stability under the Celtic church (which Gunn later celebrated by applauding the reconstruction of Iona).

Sun Circle's rooting about in a religion of blood-letting and sexual instinctualism seems to share common ground with D H Lawrence and this may be another link to *After Strange Gods*, in part a critique of Lawrence's fiction. The association of brutality with a lack of religious background altogether is perhaps the main theme of *After Strange Gods*. The book was one of Eliot's most controversial works because he suggested that one of the most important elements of an individual's development was "unity of religious background", and it followed that, for example, "reasons of race and religion combine to make any large number of free-thinking Jews undesirable". This, on the face of it, is a chilling remark, (indeed Eliot seems to have regretted it since he never re-issued *After Strange Gods*). Yet the context suggests that it is the liberalism of freethinking Jews, not their Jewishness which concerns him: an attack on theological and intellectual liberalism, the 'modern heresy' of the sub-title, constitutes a significant part of the book. Eliot's conservatism is bound up with a paradoxical respect for a multiplicity of orthodoxies (with a frank admission that he believed a Christian way of life to be the best hope for the Western world!). This critique of society and societies not so much disintegrating as becoming universally mediocre is the point of contact between Gunn and Eliot.

Nationalism and literature

Having used Eliot's earlier criticism to propose confidence in a Scottish use of the English language, Gunn used *After Strange Gods* to argue for the connections between nationalism and literature. It is a measure of Gunn's interest in understanding literature in intellectual, theoretical, terms that he should respond so publicly to Eliot's criticism rather than his poetry (though both Gunn and his wife knew much of Eliot's poetry by heart, and frequently quoted it out loud). Gunn's use of the poet's theory is marked, however, by a deliberate nationalist flavour, a tincture not always apparent in Eliot. In 'President of Eire: the True Value of Tradition', he quotes Eliot's assessment in *After Strange Gods* of Joyce as "the most ethically orthodox of the more eminent writers of my time," binding this with Eliot's definitions of orthodoxy and tradition to assert that it is in part to do with Ireland's political renaissance that Joyce and other Irish writers are as good as they are:

> It is not entirely fortuitous that writers out of that Ireland which has fought so strenuously in recent times for the right to continue its own traditions should hold such a commanding position in letters to-day. Take four Irish writers representing amongst them poetry, prose and drama – W B Yeats, James Joyce, George Bernard Shaw and Sean O'Casey. Is there any name in the whole realm of English literature to-day that one could prefer before them? It is a thought to meditate upon.

Here Gunn appropriates the Irish writers, with the seeming approval of Eliot, as a creative product of the successful Irish revival and revolution, asserting that they are living proof of a connection between confidence in one's own traditions and the quality of the new cultural phenomena that such a society produces. He extends the principle to bread-and-butter issues, citing the success of Ireland's Shannon Power Scheme, and noting drily the failure of the Caledonian Hydro-Electric project to even get started.

If Gunn is making questionable assertions about Joyce's reliance on Irish traditions, he is dissembling on a larger scale in his rendering of Eliot. This is his quotation of Eliot:

> When T S Eliot, writing of James Joyce, calls him 'the most ethically orthodox of the more eminent writers of my time', he is aware of Joyce as the product of his Irish environment. Indeed, tradition and orthodoxy are complementary to Eliot. 'I hold... that a *tradition* is rather a way of feeling and acting which characterises a group throughout generations; and that it must largely be, or that many of the elements in it must be, unconscious; whereas the maintenance of *orthodoxy* is a matter which calls for the exercise of all our conscious intelligence. The two will, therefore, considerably complement each other... Tradition may be conceived as a by-product of right living, not to be aimed at directly. It is of the blood, so to speak, rather than of the brain; it is the means by which the vitality of the past enriches the life of the present. In the co-operation of both is the reconciliation of thought and feeling.'
>
> Tradition is not a static thing; it is a living growth. And I have mentioned these two writers, who have probably had a greater influence on modern letters than any other two one could readily think of in the world to-day, because they are popularly held to be revolutionary and unorthodox.

Though the first ellipsis is a relatively innocent one, omitting only "in summing up", and therefore removing the sense that a careful and more detailed argument has proceeded before it, the second cut is major surgery. This is what Eliot says in those three little dots:

> The two will therefore considerably complement each other. Not only is it possible to conceive of a tradition being definitely bad; a good tradition might, in changing circumstances, become out of date. Tradition has not the means to criticise itself; it may perpetuate much that is trivial or of transient significance as well as what is vital and permanent. And while tradition, being a matter of good habits, is necessarily real only in a social group, orthodoxy exists whether realised in anyone's thought or not. Orthodoxy also, of course represents a concensus between the living and the dead: but a whole generation might conceivably pass without any orthodox thought; or, as by Athanasius, orthodoxy may be upheld by one man against the world. Tradition may be conceived as a by-product of right living

This cut is a deliberate avoidance of what Eliot admitted were the *bad* aspects of tradition; mention of the autonomous nature of orthodoxy is also excised. It is not difficult to see why Gunn made the change. Tradition is simplified and receives a wholly clean bill of health, and orthodoxy is not revealed in the more idiosyncratic definition Eliot gives, with its complications of being *independent* of culture and having a messy congress between the dead and the living (made messier by mention of an obscure fourth century saint). Thus de-complicated , the text produces the right platform for Gunn to make the assertion that Eliot and Joyce are, contrary to popular perception, as unrevolutionary (traditional) and orthodox as they are perceived to be "revolutionary and unorthodox" – and this, Gunn asserts, is to their credit. They have advanced their respective traditions rather than broken from them. It is not a large step from assuming that Gunn is identifying with Joyce and Eliot, either: that, from the standpoint of his own perceived literary tradition, he, too, has moved things on.

The Modern Mind and *Wild Geese Overhead*

The clearest use of Eliot's criticism in Gunn's fiction takes place in *Wild Geese Overhead* (1939). The glimpses of Scottish cities in novels as early as *The Poaching at Grianan* give way here to Gunn's most comprehensive depiction of Scottish urban life. Though the location is Glasgow it is never named as such: it is like Muir's and Kafka's urban worlds, the universal city. Nevertheless, the shipyards and steamers, the football, the slums, trams, and socialism, and the history of its working class activism – "Did any city in the world ever put up such a fight for workers' rights as this city did?" – and even a snatch of dialect, make sure we know where we are. A sense of richness and complexity within both the working and middle classes is ably conveyed. While Gunn fails, I think, by almost totally ignoring the spoken language of Glasgow (no small omission), there is a sense, as there is not in the later Glasgow novel *The Lost Chart* (1949), that the city here is more a subject in itself, rather than a useful context for another debate.

The main figure in the book, Will, is a sub-editor, journalist, and reviewer, primarily attached to the evening paper. It is as a reviewer that he becomes fascinated by Eliot's literary criticism, a convenient occupation by which to introduce Gunn's literary concerns. It is interesting to note in passing that Gunn does not live up to Will's expectations of "that ultimate apprehension of truth" when he selectively quotes Eliot in 'President of Eire' in what is indeed "a special or propagandist pleading". This general statement of interest in criticism is tightened to an interest in Eliot's theory. Will admires Eliot's poetry for the way its innovative technique is underlain by a defence of tradition, and sees that defence given clear expression in the poet's prose. "For the interesting thing about Mr. Eliot was that, though regarded as the most revolutionary force in modern poetry, yet no man in his essays put up a finer case for orthodoxy and tradition.". We recognise here, with those key words "orthodoxy" and "tradition" that Gunn is, once again, responding to *After Strange Gods*.

Near the beginning of the book, Will is reading Eliot's essay, 'The Modern Mind'. It is indicative of Will's own psychological state that he is interested in Eliot's commentary on loneliness. Will's behaviour is that of a man who, intermittently, feels intensely alienated; his psychological breakdown near the end of the book seems to have more significance than the beating which precipitates it. In 'The Modern Mind' Eliot is discussing I A Richards' ideas on the reader's approach to responding poetry, and in particular his list of topics to think about if one is unsure how to interpret a particular poem. The first on the list is "Man's loneliness (the isolation of the human situation)", a notion about which Eliot is sceptical. In the original:

> I. Man's loneliness (the isolation of the human situation)
>
> Loneliness is known as a frequent attitude in romantic poetry, and in the form of 'lonesomeness' (as I need not remind American readers) is a frequent attitude in contemporary lyrics known as 'the blues'. But in what sense is Man in general isolated, and from what? What *is* the 'human situation'? I can understand the isolation of the human situation as Plato's Diotima expounds it, or in the Christian sense of the separation of Man from God; but not an isolation which is not a separation from anything in particular.

In the novel Gunn cuts Eliot's comments down, presenting them like this:

> (1) Man's loneliness (the isolation of the human situation)
>
> And promptly underneath it came Mr. Eliot's comment: "Loneliness is a frequent attitude in contemporary lyrics known as 'the blues'..."
>
> Will laughed, as if he could hardly believe it!
>
> Restless, he laid the book aside and lit a cigarette. Was he going to get a slant on Eliot's vulnerability through his blind spot (even if deliberately blind)?

Now that "promptly underneath it" is only half-true: Gunn cuts out mention of romantic poetry and "lonesomeness" to go straight to the blues. This emphasises the modernity of what Eliot is describing, but Gunn's final ellipsis disguises Eliot's whole point: that he cannot conceive "an isolation which is not a separation from anything in particular." However, Will seems to see Eliot's recognition of loneliness in modern forms of expression as revealing Eliot's "vulnerability". He can laugh at Eliot's pomposity, but it is Will's *general* sense of loneliness that dominates the book: he *does* feel "isolated" without feeling isolated from anything in particular.

'The Modern Mind' may have contributed to the imagery used in the novel as well as to the thematic framework. In the essay Eliot confirms I A Richards' observation "that Canto XXVI of the *Purgatorio* illuminates 'my persistent concern with sex, the problem of our generation, as religion was the problem of the last.'" Agreeing that the *Purgatorio* has been personally important, Eliot refutes the assumption that either sex or religion is a transient concern. In doing so he draws attention to the prominence of sex and religion throughout history. In Canto XXVI these themes entwine, as in *Wild Geese Overhead*. In Canto XXVI Dante encounters those who had been lustful when alive. The inhabitants here are not eternally damned, however. Like Gunn's city-dwellers, whose world is described in terms of a hellish underworld, they are marked out (usually) by their warm-heartedness. Many of those in the novel's Glasgow who have "sinned", have done so in concupiscence rather than malice, and for them there is not a sense of utter hopelessness. The novel is indeed a series of erotic trials – from Will's bus conductress, the prositute Ivy, the liberated socialite Felicity, to the secretary, Jenny, with which Will is finally united. The allegorical nature of the *Divine Comedy* reminds one, too, that Will (whose very name suggests allegorical significance) is a modern pilgrim who fights off nihilism and sexual incontinence to win through to his own state of grace. Indeed there is a strong argument for seeing *Wild Geese Overhead* as a spiritual and sexual allegory, so the normal standards for judging "realistic" novels have to be cast aside. To judge Gunn in the sole terms of realist narrative is to deny the whole mode in which his novels proceed, as if, to take a recent example in another medium, Almodovar's *Matador* should be seen as failing to be a realistic study of bull-fighting!

If 'The Modern Mind' had been used to supply an intellectual sanction of interest in what happens to Will, towards the end of the novel, argument from *The Use of Poetry and the Use of Criticism* is used to suggest a way of transcending the nihilism Will has been trying to fight back. Will focuses on Eliot's description of poetry written in illness, which Eliot describes as a "*negative*" release of one's persistent anxieties, and points out that the poetic product of this impulse (in Eliot's own admission) is indistinguishable from that produced by "inspiration". He wonders if a way of writing could be found that would place and transform experience, "negative" or "positive", into art of the highest order. Drawing from this notion of the poetic product being divorced from its creative impulse, and following Richards' idea of a "technique of sincerity" for *responding* to poetry, he asks: "Why not develop a technique for any experience that had already proved real and that depended for its repetition solely on the individual mind?".

Because Gunn has brought Eliot's discussion of writing poetry into contact with Eliot's discussion of appreciating it, it is unclear to what side of the poetry process Will is referring – whether creation or appreciation. Indeed, it is as if Will is looking for a general theory for the whole creative process – and it seems safe to say that there is sufficient sympathy between character and author to state that Gunn is here expounding his own poetic. That poetic is based on actual experience, on facts, on autobiography – "any experience that had already proved real". As Hart and Pick's biography shows, Gunn's fiction arises from a skilled assembling and re-expression of such "real-life" episodes, but there is also a sense of *validation* in Gunn's use of the phrase "proved real". This technique of writing/responding to literature (I take the liberty of widening the debate from poetry) is to be founded on not just any occurence, but an occurence which was of intrinsic significance. In other words, Will is proposing a selective form of literary collage whose constituent parts are themselves of importance and do not merely derive their importance from the association within which they are ultimately placed by the artist (one brings to one's response experience that is in some sense "meaningful" in its own right).

Now this brings us closer to what Gunn means by "proved real". The kernel of this is what is usually called "mystical" by his critics. Eliot uses this term, not dismissively, but to distinguish it from the experience of writing poetry, but Will wishes to blur the distinction:

> Will smiled, and when Mr. Eliot went on to find his experience 'a very different thing from mystical illumination' he immediately doubted that 'very different'. What did he mean by "mystical illumination' anyhow? When was illumination in the mind 'mystical'? When one thought of God or something high and mighty? But nonsense, because the final feat of the mystic was to realize his deeper self, to apprehend it calmly in a condition of light. It was this light or illumination that mattered.

Gunn can only go so far with Will's definitions. While the idea of "light or illumination" is verbally intangible, it exemplifies the wordless state of being with which Gunn is interested (or, as in *The Other Landscape*, the W S Graham-like fascination in that uneven membrane separating language and meaning). But he has given us a glimpse of the technique through which these illuminations are rendered fiction. Using facts from his own experience and research, almost indeed as Eliot uses allusions and samples of other texts, Gunn rearranges and reembeds that experience to create work which, "like Mr. Eliot's "automatic writing", seemed to produce itself." As Eliot draws from high and low culture, Gunn uses folk art, folk history, and first-hand testimony – but only so long as it has validity in itself. Gunn's response to Eliot's theory, therefore, is to help define the ideas behind his own fiction, and to indicate how far those ideas can be defined.

Gunn and the use of criticism

The aura of the Scottish Renaissance radiated into the wider community of ideas in the inter-war years. Though the connections between the Renaissance and the modernists outwith Scotland were reciprocal they are exemplified by the influence of Eliot's criticism on Gunn's thinking. In *After Strange Gods* Eliot made the connection between the Renaissance and the southern American Agrarian movement. *The Green Isle of the Great Deep* (1944), for instance, reads now like a companion to the break up of Eastern Europe so clearly does Gunn understand the nature of freedom and that of bureaucratic authoritarianism.

.   Though Gunn felt ambivalent towards the self-consciousness and "difficult" techniques of the modernists, his use of Eliot's criticism indicates that he nevertheless interpreted himself as having close thematic and intellectual affinities with the foremost. He also used Eliot's criticism in the cause of Scottish independence, a use which exemplifies his belief that literature and how we interpret it *matters*. In emphasising the urgent connection between culture and the individuals that produce and are produced by it, Gunn's voice still speaks with intelligence for today.

Richard Price

FIFTH ESTATE

SEASON 1992-1993

Country Dance by James Kennaway

Dundee Repertory Theatre, March 11-28

The Jesuit by Donald Campbell

Netherbow Theatre, Edinburgh, April 28-May 16
Perth Festival, May 21-23; The Tron, Glasgow, May 26-31

Kepler by Robert Forrest

Edinburgh Festival Fringe
Netherbow Theatre, August 12-September 5

The Consul of Butterflies by Bernard da Costa

(Transl. Lorna Irvine)
Netherbow Theatre, October/November dates T.B.C.

La Serva Amorosa by Carlo Goldoni

(Where Love Steps In)
Transl. and adapted by Antonia Stott and Margery Greig
Netherbow Theatre, December dates T.B.C.

The Scapegoat by Clive Paton

The New Traverse Theatre, Edinburgh
February 1993, Dates T.B.C.

"THEATRE WORTH WATCHING"

Socialism and Self-Determination in the City Novels of Neil Gunn

Margery McCulloch

Neil Gunn is not typically a novelist of the city. While his most characteristic books develop his sense of essential Highland experience, the city, when it enters into his fiction, often appears as a source of degeneration and loss of humanity, a negative perspective which is consistently set in opposition to the virtue of the Highlands and their traditional rural values. Yet while this view is true of Gunn's work when considered as a whole, I have come increasingly to realise that it does encourage one to sideline a number of significant city experiences dramatised in his fiction.

Gunn's reputation as a novelist was made in the 1930s and 40s, but *The Serpent* (1943) reminds us how closely by date of birth he was allied to the Victorian period. With its earliest scenes set in the 1880s, the book displays the late Victorian preoccupation with an increasingly militant socialism, often allied to atheism; and with prostitution – "Antichrist and the Scarlet Woman", as the principal character Tom ironically designates the public's undifferentiated perception of such twin social evils.

For Tom, however, as for many working people of the time, socialism was no evil, but a new and liberating faith: a faith which offered the possibility of ameliorating the wretched conditions of slum-dwellers and other deprived working people in the here and now. This early socialist idealism, with its revolutionary fervour and religious sense of social mission, provided also the intellectual means by which one could throw off the "mind-forg'd manacles" diagnosed previously by Blake and Shelley in their revolutionary poetry. The excitement and exhilaration of this new way forward is dramatised through Tom's first contact with Glasgow and its socialist community.

A country lad from a Highland village, Tom goes to the city to work as an assistant in a hardware shop. Through a lucky mishap he is able to demonstrate his skill in working with machinery and is transferred from the situation of counter assistant to workroom apprentice. This is no chance detail in the action. For Gunn in this novel, Tom's machine skills, his precise working methods and his pride in completing a task to his own satisfaction, epitomise the new skilled working man and his independence.

Tom's mentor is Dougal, the head of the workshop, "a first-class craftsman and conscientious in so austere a way that it struck Tom at first as being almost religious." It is through Dougal also that Tom first learns to use not only his hands but his mind and to question the 'Idols of the Tribe': "Huxley. Darwin. Robert Owen. Haeckel. Oh, the excitement in those days! Impossible for this late age ever to recapture that first fearful delight, that awful thrill, of Scepticism." Tom learns to examine the history of his own Highland people as well as that of the urban working class. He realises for the first time the full iniquity of the Clearances, the economic circumstances which fuelled them and the cruelty with which they were carried out. He begins to question the restrictive and socially conditioned interpretations of Christianity put about by the ministers who, particularly in the country communities, still monitored and directed the lives of the people. He comes to understand that there are some people who do not seem to see the need to question accepted ideologies or attempt to take charge of their own lives.

Prostitution is a complementary social motif: the atmosphere of menace in the Victorian city is communicated through Tom's encounter with a prostitute on the dark night streets. Just as his intellectual naïvete was highlighted in his early encounters with Dougal's socialist ideology, so his sexual inexperience is emphasised in his innocent meeting with the prostitute. In *Wild Geese Overhead*, the more sophisticated city journalist Will attempts to include the prostitute in his embrace of the deprived and rejected, but here in *The Serpent* she takes into herself all the horror and menace of the unfamiliar city nightscape. As Tom flees from the streetwoman, the city seems to threaten him less on account of its sordid slums and the explosive violence they potentially contain than as a symbol of human impulses which cannot yet be brought out into the light and examined objectively as the socialists were now examining the economic forces within society. Tom's fear of the prostitute is the fear of the lust arising in himself.

Despite the underside of city life seen through Tom's night adventure, *The Serpent* on the whole presents a strong case for the positives of the city experience in the areas of self-education and political awareness, and this is brought out nowhere more forcibly than in the account of Tom's return to his village after the illness of his father. While in Gunn's novels of Highland boyhood one is conscious of the security the community and its traditions give to the growing boy, the community's capacities for fulfilment are not tested beyond the boyhood stage. In *The Serpent* this silence in the text is given voice. Tom's workshop becomes the meeting place for the young men of the village, who are fascinated by his free thinking no less than by his skill with mechanical tools. His elders, on the other hand, cannot accommodate him. He is slandered, then ostracised, an atheistical serpent in their midst, come to break the people's beliefs and destroy the philosophical and social *status quo*. Although Tom modifies and questions some of his Glasgow attitudes as he matures and experiences life more fully, he does not relinquish the freedom to explore and question, to throw off the intellectual manacles which an isolated, inward-looking community, dominated by a severe, fundamentalist religion, can impose on its members. The city experience in this book, as in *The Drinking Well*, is a necessary route to self-determination.

Wild Geese Overhead (1939), although pre-dating *The Serpent*, takes the ideological debate beyond the initial religious fervour and optimism of the early socialists towards a more objective critique of the system. The opposition here is between a rational, utilitarian adherence to "the cause" on the one hand, and an insistence on the need for the individual response at all costs on the other, the latter being the view of the novel's main character, Will, a city journalist who decides to take lodgings in the countryside in an attempt to achieve spiritual restoration.

The overall context of the novel is that of the late 1930s, when the Spanish Civil War was in progress and fears of a wider European conflict omnipresent. A sense of inevitability and hopelessness dominates the pub talk between Will and his fellow journalists. "You get worn down by this eternal mess ... It's a sort of mass-hypnosis of all the people in the world, a belief that what they all loathe is yet inevitable." And socialism no longer seems the obvious answer: "Change the system and we'll all be nice fellows? If every country in the world was a socialist state there would be no war? Quite. But first of all, our country isn't a socialist state. And secondly, the countries likely to win the war will be the best organised countries militarily. The strongest iron hand will rule the peace. What chance do you see of a true socialism emerging from a war between the present alignment of the 'crisis' countries? In our time?"

Although as a journalist Will has had previous superficial contact with the city slums, his first real initiation is through his socialist acquaintance Joe who takes him into the heart of the city's deprived underworld to visit a pregnant woman and her husband, an unemployed carpenter who has recently lost his right arm in an industrial accident about which there is a compensation dispute. Faced with the inequalities and iniquities of the capitalist system as it affects the slum-dwellers, Will is forced to examine his own ideas about the nature of socialism and the 'freedom' of the individual.

For, in addition to his disillusionment with socialism's inability to transform the system, Will is unsettled in relation to what he perceives as the intrinsic anti-individualistic nature of socialism. And in this concern he speaks to a large extent for Gunn himself. In the 1941 article, 'Memories of the Months: a Balance Sheet', Gunn reviewed a series of essays on the countryside which he had written for the *Scots Magazine* in these early years of the war, and defended his turning to Nature and "away from the dread realities that encompass us", this attempt of the individual to "break free from the concerns of the mass." It is this question of the individual's need to break free from a mass ideology which concerned him in his relations with both socialism and capitalism. He saw that what had come to dominate both systems, and to dominate even more fiercely in a time of war, was what he called "a corporate consciousness of the herd ... the great modern heresy." As we find in Gunn's novels of Highland experience, his ideal is for a co-operative, communal form of society. But for him the individual is at the heart of society, and it is this individual contribution which enables the co-operative social patterns to work successfully; not the suppression of individuality and the acknowledgement of the individual as "a unit in the mass", as he believed was becoming increasingly the case in the modern urban world. Gunn's view is that "we cannot conceive of a symphony being composed by society"; if that were ever to happen, then "at that moment individual inspiration will have died, as it died in the beehive."

The arguments between Joe and Will in *Wild Geese Overhead* can be seen to be the forerunners of Gunn's stance in 'Memories of the Months' and also in the later novel *The Green Isle of the Great Deep*, where the central theme is the validity and vitality of the individual life as opposed to the quiescent conformity to a mass ideology developed, supposedly, for the greater good of all. The problem highlighted in *Wild Geese Overhead* is that faced with the utter deprivation and desperation of the slum-dwellers, concern about the freedom of the individual *not* to conform retreats before the need for a system which will identify and alleviate the conditions of the slum-dwelling masses. Joe's argument is the utilitarian one put forward by Robert Owen in the 19th century when he set up his New Lanark community, namely that "no individual is free. He is a product of and is conditioned by his social relations." Given this ideology, Joe sees the aim of his socialist creed as being to run society in such a way as to "eliminate its shocking miseries and tyrannies and botched economics, that the individual in the socialist society will be in a far better position to contribute the maximum that's in him and so help society forward to a degree that's never been seen before."

Will, however, is not fully satisfied: "when you shift the emphasis from the individual to society, to social relations, you shift it from the vivid springing core of life to a windy, if convenient abstraction. But, and this is the snag: it is *difficult* to be a real individual living from your feet up. It needs grit, and pride, and courage, and power to endure through despair; you need to be quick with beauty, and light, and love, and sex; you must see men, not as social units, but as your individual brothers, full of this magic thing called life. And this is difficult. But – it is *easy* to be a socialist, it is easy to cry for ideal justice and go forward as one in the ranks ... " In the context of the narrative's previous excursion into the slums, and the account of Will's inability to cope with what he sees, it is Joe's answer which seems unanswerable: "Had it not been for the cause, I should not have done what I had done? Possibly. What is certain is that had it not been for the cause I should not have known them at all, and so have done nothing."

The issues, both local and international, which Gunn explored in a variety of essays and novels in the 1930s and 1940s continue to have validity in our late 20th century world, and nowhere is this more so than in the field of social and political ideology. In the last two years we have seen the collapse of communism in the countries of Eastern Europe and have rejoiced over the new 'freedom' available to their peoples. Yet who among us can be entirely happy with some of the forms which this so-called freedom is taking, with the resurfacing of old prejudices and enmities, with the continued – and in some case increased – economic deprivation suffered by the people of the former Eastern Bloc. Will's instinct for the 'free spirit' is a sound one, but so is Joe's understanding that without some ideological economic and social basis the lives of the deprived masses cannot be improved and their capacity to express their free spirits will of necessity remain stunted. The urban setting of *Wild Geese Overhead* foregrounds the paradoxical nature of this dilemma in a way that the Highland narratives with their simpler social context and depiction of traditional values cannot.

Some of the most vital writing in this novel is to be found in the descriptions of the slum areas and of Will's response to what he encounters there. The woman Ettie has died in childbirth; Joe and Will search for her husband Jamie in the alleys and pubs down by the river. Interacting with his fears for Jamie's safety as they search "down past the building yards ... where all the men worked whose forefathers had made the river, the river of seaborne traffic, the wonder river", Will cannot suppress irritation that this city should have so neglected its environmental as well as its human potential. As they walked along the river, "they could not see it. Why shouldn't they be able to see it? Why should it be banked in, shut away? Why should there not be boulevards along it?" For this man-made city has become a thing of ugliness for the workers who have to live along its river banks, a manmade desolation in contrast to the garden suburbs of its West End.

The stench of the city oppresses the reader no less than Will, the stench of shared lavatories, of unaired, overcrowded rooms, of the sickness of illness and the sickness of drink-induced vomit, the stench of drains and disease. As in *The Serpent*, debased sex is part of the city nightmare, although Will's encounters with the prostitute Ivy are more ludicrous than menacing. The menace here is in the overcrowded living conditions with their encouragement of unlawful relationships, in the sexual precociousness of the foul-mouthed children, in the poverty that makes what we consider 'normal' family living impossible. Coming back to this novel after a number of years and a previous harsh appraisal of it, I have been struck freshly by the power of its depiction of the city underworld, an uncharacteristic milieu for Gunn and one which belongs with Edwin Muir's accounts of Glasgow slums in books such as *An Autobiography, Scottish Journey* and the novel *Poor Tom*. I still find the novel formally unsatisfactory when taken as a whole, and the author's apparent endorsement of the weaker elements of Will's characterisation threatens to subvert the significant debates between Will and Joe on the nature of freedom. Nevertheless, in the raising of these ideological issues and in the strength of its depiction of the city slums, *Wild Geese Overhead* is a book of continuing relevance.

My final city experience is that of *The Drinking Well* (1946) which has as its principal setting a sheep farm in the Grampians and an overall theme which involves the regeneration of the Highlands through enlightened management. The city depicted in this book is Edinburgh and the ideological debate carried out in that city focusses on the way forward for Scotland as a nation: should Scotland's regeneration be through socialism, as the political orator Davidson claims, or should it be through nationalism, as advocated by the historian and lawyer Douglas? Gunn set the book in the inter-war period when debates about Scottish cultural and economic regeneration were very much to the fore. On the other hand, in the passages relating to sheep farming and the Highlands, one senses that he is taking advantage of the moves toward economic change in the Highlands which were beginning to be set in motion in the immediate post-war period when the book was being written and when the new Labour government with Scottish Secretary of State Tom Johnston was attempting to set an alternative economic agenda.

The situation of the principal character Iain is a recurring one in Gunn's fiction: namely that of the young man sent out of the Highlands to make his career in the important world of the south. Gunn spent two years in Edinburgh between 1909 and late 1911. He catches acutely the atmosphere of legal offices and private schooling, of privilege and sophisticated know-how in business and personal relationships; catches too the awkwardness and social clumsiness of the young Highlander who initially finds himself a country yokel in the eyes of his new colleagues and personal acquaintances. The depiction of establishment Edinburgh sets the context for the arguments to come. One can understand how this comfortable society, with its privileges but absence of any real responsibility, would not care to have its existence threatened by socialism or nationalism.

But Edinburgh, middle class or deprived, cannot in reality escape its history. On his arrival, Iain, gazing up at the Castle "was caught into history … and he felt in himself the smallness of individual life against that which endures." In the slum areas of the old town where he wanders with the lawyer and historian Douglas down the once Royal Mile towards the Palace of Holyrood, he again comes up against history, "the ancient, the stormy, the gay and gallant and dark and bloody pageant of Scots history." Douglas is a romantic, passionately attached to every stone of Scotland's past and sure that this history is the only basis on which to move forward. Yet his vital interest in the past seems to lose specificity whenever it comes close to the problems of the present. Iain comes to suspect that Douglas is getting drunk in the past because there is no glorious present or future to get drunk in.

As Tom in *The Serpent* had his education at the hands and mind of the socialist Dougal, so in *The Drinking Well* Iain is first brought to think rationally about Scotland's situation through his listening to the socialist orator Davidson at the Mound. He finds Davidson's "matter-of-fact way of dealing with the ancient subject of Scottish nationhood" appeals to his mind and encourages him to think in a similar way about his homeland and its problems. Like MacDiarmid's Drunk Man, who "micht ha'e been contentit wi' the Rose/ Gin I'd had ony reason to suppose/ That what the English dae can e'er mak' guid/ For what Scots dinna – and first and foremaist should", so the socialist Douglas asks why we should blame the English for Scotland's situation when the fault "lay 'in ourselves'? If the people of Scotland wanted to take their derelict country in hand, to govern and rebuild it, no power on earth could stop them from doing so – and certainly not the English! Scotland had the resources, she had the wealth, she was capable of developing one of the most perfectly balanced and richest economies in Europe. Yet what did we find everywhere? Unemployed, stagnant yards, derelict areas, slums, depopulation, with the young men and women leaving the crofts, leaving the farms, leaving the sea, to emigrate or to come to a city like this." In these arguments we can hear Gunn himself talking, as in his many *Scots Magazine* articles on the condition of the Highlands, his pleas for "belief in ourselves" and a new economic strategy for the Highlands. And these are the arguments which first excite Iain's imagination and send him to investigate the detail of Scotland's economic and social history.

Just as Will could not be completely satisfied with Joe's socialist position in *Wild Geese Overhead*, there is in Iain and his author the awareness of another argument which needs to be taken account of so far as the revitalisation of Scotland is concerned. For Gunn himself, as we see in his articles and novels about Highland life, the way forward was through "growing and blossoming from our own roots" in the past. And this is a dimension which does not seem to concern Davidson so closely. As Joe declared in *Wild Geese* that without the socialist cause he would never have known about the need of Ettie and Jamie and so could not possibly have helped them, so Davidson argues that "without bread man cannot live at all." For him, Scotland must revive economically before the matter of cultural revival and nationhood can be addressed.

This is not Gunn's way, however. In *The Drinking Well* he puts the case for cultural revival into the mouth of the historian Douglas. The discussions take the course which one feels the talks with MacDiarmid which Gunn remembers in the short article 'For Christopher's Cap' must have taken. Is there such a thing as "a distinctive Scottish capacity for creativity in the arts?" Is Scotland the only country which is not capable of a distinctive historical and psychological expression of the human spirit? Davidson the socialist agrees that Scotland is no less potentially capable of this than any other country in the world – but what he sees as incontrovertible is that "before you can do anything about a country's creativity on the world level, that country must first of all be in a position to control her own affairs."

Others in the discussion feel that this is not a necessary condition, that a "modern literature in Scotland" can be produced "in the existing circumstances" and "without any direct reference" to the past. Davidson, despite his insistence that economic regeneration must come first, understands more clearly that "literature as indeed all the arts, is in its highest form held to be an expression of what you call the unconscious. Its expression is made, of course, through the intellect, but its power derives directly from the unconscious. And the unconscious, I understand, is the sum of our past". Again we can hear Gunn himself speaking. What is ultimately seen to be necessary is the bringing together of the economic and cultural arguments: "a country grows out of its past as a man out of his childhood." The past cannot be denied without irretrievable loss. But neither can the need to find an economic and political solution for the present and future.

As in the socialist/free spirit arguments in *Wild Geese Overhead* there are no definite conclusions reached in the economic/cultural debate of *The Drinking Well*. Yet, in company with the ideological debates of the other city novels, the questions argued out in this book are still of vital importance to Scotland's future – and are in the main still unresolved. Scotland would seem to have chosen Davidson's socialist road, but it is a choice subverted by the lack of self-determination and therefore by the imposition of a quite different political and economic philosophy from London. We are, I think, seeing a distinctive Scottish form of expression in the arts nowadays, an expression which feels able to call on the past, where relevant, without being bound or restricted by it. Yet side by side with this revival and confidence is the awareness that in a social sense our distinctive forms of speech and customs are being steadily eroded as the blandness of television conditions our interests and there continues to be no stable centre or anchoring point in Scotland for the nurturing of the cultural revival which has been taking place since Gunn and MacDiarmid argued out the case for a Scottish renaissance. Too often our arts administrators and decision-makers – often coming from outwith the country – attempt to propagate their ideas about how international culture should be presented, but have no proper understanding of the distinctive, indigenous culture which they find here. This is a problem which Gunn instinctively understood and argued out in the 1930s when he insisted that the move outwards to true internationalism must be based on an understanding of one's own culture.

While Neil Gunn is therefore not characteristically a novelist of the city, it is the city experience which offered him the most fertile context for the intellectual arguments about cultural and economic renewal and the ideological question of how to combine some form of socialism with the retention of freedom for the individual. It is a measure of his significance as a writer, both within Scotland and internationally, and a fitting tribute to him in his centenary year that the issues which he debated in his essays and novels of the 1930s and 1940s continue to be of relevance to our late 20th century world.   **Margery McCulloch**

*A scene from the film of **The Silver Darlings**, Holyrood Productions, 1947 (National Library of Scotland)*

*Neil M Gunn interviewd by Maurice Lindsay for the **Scottish Field**, 1960 (John Watt)*

Neil Gunn and Nationalism: A memoir

Neil MacCormick

Neil Gunn's passionate commitment to a Scottish vision of the human predicament shines from all he wrote. Whatever his party political allegiances might have turned out to be, there is an obvious sense in which the author of *Morning Tide* could not but be called a nationalist writer, albeit with a noticeably small 'n', and with a markedly universalistic vision through the intensely observed particular. But in a formal way, it was my father, John MacCormick, who first recruited Gunn to Scottish nationalism in a politically committed sense. The year was 1929, the National Party of Scotland (not till 1932, 'Scottish National Party') was but a year old. MacCormick, then 25, was deputed, or rather deputed himself, as Party secretary to organise a mass meeting in Inverness that autumn to initiate a Highland campaign for Scottish nationalism.

The Town Hall was booked, with a capacity of four or five hundred, the meeting widely advertised in the local press. On the night, however, but twenty-six turned up, too scattered about the space available even to applaud the speakers. But among those present were Gunn and Duncan H McNeill (lawyer and subsequently constitutional historian of Scotland, translator of Buchanan's *De Jure Regni*). They became the core of a vigorous nationalist organisation, which came to hold many more meetings with vastly greater success than at the inauspicious beginning of the Highland campaign.

Friendships made then were long-enduring. When the Scottish Covenant campaign of 1949-50 was at its height, people were continually coming about my parents' house doing the business of the Covenant, eager with the anticipations of that remarkable period, as convinced as so many now are again that a Scots Parliament could not be long delayed after the securing of two million signatories to the Covenant. I remember clearly, with the vividness attaching to the recollections of a nine year old allowed out of bed very late to witness great things, the night that Neil Gunn and various other stalwarts, among them Robert Gray and William Whyte (deeply involved also in the Stone of Destiny affair, though that was not a fact known to me then), sat talking late into the night as I sat half hidden at the edge of the circle watching and listening. I remember more the mood and the passion than the words of those present, a mood expressed with a strangely sombre vitality by Gunn, quite the most striking person in the room with his curly grey hair, gaunt features, hollow eyes. As impressionable as I was, I felt myself in the presence of greatness and of great events in that meeting.

I remember again as a student in 1961, just before my father's death, begging from Gunn an essay for a Glasgow student magazine *Ossian*, organ of Glasgow University's Highland Students' Society. He replied that he had been going to refuse, till he read the sentence in which I gave him compliments from my parents. He gave me a characteristically allusive piece about the reseeding of common grazings in the Outer Hebrides, with an obvious but not overdone symbolism about a still-to-be-hoped-for revitalisation of the life of our rural (and maybe also urban) communities.

By that time, as a student in Philosophy with English Literature (which one could then re-interpret as to about half as Scottish Literature), I had almost independently become an admirer and avid reader of Gunn's work. I say 'almost independently', for after all I happened to live in a house where all Gunn's novels were available on the bookshelves, and was reared by admirers of his writing. But I had come to my own personal appreciation of the books, and at the time he had not been widely 'rediscovered' by the scholarly community. So my undergraduate essays interpreting Gunn and Gibbon in the light of Kurt Wittig's then-recent study of Scottish Literature maybe had a certain novelty or even originality. In context, I felt it all the more of a literary coup to have got our greatest living prose writer to contribute to *Ossian*, even if I had done a little influence-broking to get it.

Gunn's writing remains a key part in my conception of Scotland and of a civilised response to our sense of our own country and its reasonable rights alongside those of others. A recent re-reading of my father's *The Flag in the Wind* (London, Gollancz, 1955, chapter 8) has, I'm afraid, again brought home to me my unoriginality in this. For a memoir of Neil Gunn's contribution to the national movement in Scotland, I can do no better than end with an extended quotation. Speaking of the campaigning that arose out of the unpromising start in 1929, John MacCormick said this:

> I loved those Highland campaigns and the new companionship which developed from them. Neil Gunn's house in Inverness, Larachan it was called, became our unofficial headquarters and no matter how late our return from distant parts we would find him waiting for us, eager for our report and ready to sit up talking with us till all hours. As an Exciseman he was precluded from speaking at our meetings, and, in any case, his own preference was to avoid the limelight, but, behind the scenes, he inspired us with a clear vision of the Scotland that should be.
>
> Our talks ranged over the whole field of Nationalism and far beyond. We used to remark that as soon as the clock struck four in the morning we would find ourselves discussing the most abstract problems of the human soul and its relationship to God. Whether these discussions on that high plane ever reached any very definite conclusion is doubtful but there is no doubt that we began to formulate the ideas which have to a very large extent guided the development of the national movement in Scotland and, as I believe, made it something quite distinct and different from any parallel movement in other submerged European nations.
>
> We had no hatred or even of dislike for things English nor did we labour under any deep sense of grievance or injustice ... It seemed obvious to us ... that the submersion of Scotland in an incorporating Union with England was not only bad for Scotland but was also detrimental to the well-being of the whole island and of Europe too. It was as though what should have been a quartet in the concert of nations had degenerated into a one-man band.   **Neil MacCormick**

uirsgeul

le crisdean whyte

myth : poems in gaelic
with english translations

ISBN 1 871901 06 5   £8.70

GAIRM, 29 WATERLOO STREET, GLASGOW G2 6BZ, SCOTLAND

Anne Frater

Eildon

Trì beanntan a bha aonnan
mus d'thàinig am buisneachd
a rinn an sgaradh
nach gabh a chàradh

Shreap mi a chiad fhear
'nam ruith
'nam leanabh
agus shuidh mi air a mhullach
a' coimhead mo shaoghail
sgaoilt' aig mo chasan
agus an ath bheinn
faisg air làimh.

Shreap mi an dàrna cnoc
agus dh' fhàs mo chasen sgìth
Ged a bha mo shlighe furasd',
agus chaill mi m'anail;
agus bha ceò ag èirigh
a dalladh mo shealladh.
Thill mi sìos …

chuir mi mo bhoinn air an treas beinn
agus ghoid' aghaidh chas
lùths mo chasan
ged a thug e dom shùilean
sealladh farsaing gu fàire m' aineolais

Gu sgìth, gu slaodach,
chuir mi m'aghaidh ri dachaigh,
agus dòchas cadal;
ach nuair a bhuail mo bhròg
air beinn mo chiad cheum
dhùisg mo neart
agus ruith mi suas a shlios
le òran 'nam bheul.

Anne Frater

Eildon

Three peaks which were one
before the sorcery
caused the split
which cannot be repaired.

I climbed the first one
running
as a child
and I sat on the summit
regarding my world
spread out at my feet
and the next mountain
close at hand.

I climbed the second hill
and my legs grew weary
although my route was easy,
and I was out of breath,
and a mist was rising
blocking my view.
I went back down ...

I positioned my feet on the third slope
and its steep face
stole the strength from my legs
although it gave my eyes a glimpse
of the vast plains of my ignorance.

Wearily, slowly,
I turned towards home
and the hope of sleep,
but when my shoe touched
the hill of my first steps
my strength awoke
and I raced up the slope
with a song on my lips.

Aig Abaid Mhaol-Ros

Dhealbh mo sheann shùilean do chruth
air clàr gorm an adhar.
Tha do chomharradh 'nam linntinn
'nam inntin,
's mo fhreumhan cho domhainn ri do stèidjh
mo cheangal ruit cho daingeann ri cridhe Brus,
buille a' chridhe càraichte
a' brùthadh m'fhuil;
'gam bhrosnachadh
gu 'chlaidheamh a' thogail
agus cridhe na clachairean
a' ghearradh asam;
irioslachd nam manach a sheachnadh
agus m' fhuil eile a' dhùsgadh:
m' fhuil eileanach
m' fhuil Ghàidhealach.

Fhad' s a bhitheas ceudnar againn beò
cha chrùb sinn
fo smachd na Beurla.

Clag na h-abaid a' seinn gach Sàbaid,
siomain fraoich 'ga chumail
ceangailte ri clach;
an siomain fraoich a tha gam shlaodadh
bho clachan mo chrìochan,
bho clagan nan Crìochan,
's a' slaodadh cridhe Bhruis
gu' n teanga tuath
airson a neartachadh
an aghaidh òrd ùr;
airson ar cuideachadh
an damhan-allaidh a' lorg
a stiùireas sinn
gu Allt a' Bhonnaich ùr.

At Melrose Abbey

My ancient eyes drew your shape
on the blue plain of the sky.
Your mark runs through my centuries
through my mind,
and my roots are as deep as your foundations;
my bond with you as stubborn as The Bruce's heart,
the beating of his buried heart
stirring my blood;
inciting me
to raise his sword
and cut out of me
the stonemason's heart;
to shun the humility of the monks
and rouse my other blood:
my island blood
my Gaelic blood.

As long as one hundred of us remain alive
we will yield in no least way
to English dominion.

The abbey bell singing every Sunday,
a heather rope keeping it
tied to stone;
the heather rope that pulls me
from the stones of my beginnings,
from the bells of the Borders,
and pulls the heart of Bruce
to the northern tongue
to strengthen it
against a new hammer;
to help us find
the spider
which will lead us
to a new Bannockburn.

Atharrachadh

Suailean a' tighinn gu tràigh
's a' briseadh air sgian gainmhich
mar chuimhneachan air na creagan
a chaidh am mìneachadh
gu dust geur buidhe.

Caistealan creaga
air an leagail
airson lìonadh peile
agus caisteal gainmhich
a' thogail.

Neart a' ruith troimh làmhan chloinne.

Abaid Mhaol-Ros

An e mo làmhan a thog do thur?
An do gheàrr do chlachan
feòil mo fhreumhan?
Anam an fheadhainn
a thug dhomh m' ainm
sgrìobht' air do leacan
a chaidh an leagail gu làr
le naimhdeas Ghoill,
gus nach robh air fhàgail
ach do chnàmhan chraobhach
àlainn.

Sheas an tùr
an aghaidh gaoth Galld',
an aghaidh teine,
an aghaidh uisg',
's chuir iad unnad clag ùr
gus an cluinntear do ghuth
a' seinn 's a mhadainn Shàbaid.

A-mach a d' asnaichean àrsaidh
thainig eugh ùr,
agus chaneil againn a-nis
ach an nathair a sgiùrrsadh asd'.

Change

Waves coming to shore
and breaking on the sand's blade
in memory of the rocks
that were worn down
to a sharp yellow dust.

Rocky castles
demolished
to fill a pail
and build a castle
of sand.

Strength running through the hands of children.

Melrose Abbey

Were those my hands which raised your tower?
Did your stones cut
the flesh of my roots?
The soul of those
who gave me my name
written on your lintels
which were thrown to the ground
by English animosity,
until nothing was left
save your beautiful
carved skeleton.

The tower stood
in the face of foreign gales,
in the face of fire,
in the face of rain,
and they gave you a new bell
so that your voice could be heard
singing on Sunday mornings.

Out of your ancient ribs
came a new cry,
and now it only remains
for us to chase the serpent out.

An T-Airm

Cheannaicheadh do pheilear
biadh don leanabh;
gheibheadh prìs do ghunna
aodach agus brògan;
an àite do bhombaichean
sgoil agus leabhraichean
an dh'ionnsaicheadh dhà
prìsealachd sìth
Ach tha do bhombaichean
a' leagail na sgoiltean,
's do ghunna 's do pheilear
a' cuir às dha theaghlach
agus a' teagaisg dhà
fuath.

Oran

Tha do bhlas
Galld' air mo bhilean,
agus do theanga
coimheach 'nam bheul;
's ged tha do ghàirdeanan
ainnichte
gam chumail faisg,
tha fear eile a' fàs 'nam bhroinn
's nam chridhe
agus tha òran àrsaidh
gam ghluasad gu seinn.

Army

*Your bullet would buy
food for the child;
the price of your gun
would get clothing and shoes;
instead of your bombs
a school and books
which would teach him
the value of peace
But your bombs
destroy the schools
and your gun and your bullet
kill his family
and teach him
hate.*

Song

*Your taste
is foreign on my lips,
and your tongue
strange in my mouth;
and although your familiar arms
hold me close,
another grows inside my womb
and in my heart
and his ancient melody
moves me to sing.*

Anne Frater

Grassie: MacDiarmid (Edinburgh University)

HUGH MacDIARMID

1892 - 1978

A display to mark the centenary of one of Scotland's most influential and controversial writers.

NATIONAL LIBRARY OF SCOTLAND
1 - 30 April 1992
ADMISSION FREE
then touring Scotland at:

Aberdeen Central Library	7 - 22 May
Dumfries Museum	27 May - 27 June
Langholm	1 -15 July
Lanark Library	17 - 29 July
Mitchell Library, Glasgow	3 August - 12 September
MacRobert Centre, Stirling	16 September - 16 October
Inverness Museum & Art Gallery	22 October - 28 November
Montrose Library	3 December 1992 - 9 January 1993

NATIONAL
LIBRARY of
SCOTLAND

**National Library of Scotland, George IV Bridge,
Edinburgh EH1 1EW. Tel: 031-226 4531.**

The Cake

Donald Munro

When the phone rang Alex rushed through to get it. But before answering he clenched and unclenched his fists and breathed deeply, his eyes tight shut. He told himself that it would be one of the boys or a wrong number. When the receptionist spoke he sighed heavily, almost relieved that at last this was the real thing. There was nothing in her voice to hint at what was coming and as she connected the call he began to tremble and his eyes smarted. The doctor's voice, familiar from countless bedside explanations, cut in suddenly, mid-sentence: "... and so I have to tell him? Good God, it's like talking to a brick wall!"

"Bastard!" said Alex under his breath.

"Hello? What was that?" The doctor sounded all innocence.

"Me."

"Mr Macleod? Your daughter ..."

"She's got a bloody name, y'know."

"... Susan. There's been a remarkable improvement."

Alex sat down slowly on the edge of the hall table. "Improvement? Ah thought ..."

"It's quite remarkable. Sometimes it happens like this; we don't know why. She came round all by herself overnight.

"She's weak, but she asked for you. She said she wanted a piece of chocolate cake!"

Alex laughed, "Ah'll be there right away. An' Ah'll bring a cake."

His heart hammered in his chest, as if he'd been running hard. The tears were flowing now, but he was grinning. "How long till she's home?"

"Well, we still have to do some tests. And she is very weak. But she has improved a lot as you'll see."

"Ah didnae think she would ever be home."

"It was very close sometimes."

"Aye. Thanks, doctor. Look, Ah'm sorry about ..."

"Don't worry. We'll see you later."

That was it. Over. Or nearly over. He went through to the living room and sat down. He wept, loudly, without knowing why. Though there was no-one to see, he was embarrassed by his tears. Yet he felt like opening the window and shouting into the street, "She's OK! She's made it!" Before all this, it was just the kind of thing he could do. When Nancy, his ex, had left them for her man in Aberdeen, Alex had yelled out of the window after her at 11 o'clock at night. He didn't cry over her, that's for sure.

Maybe he should phone Nancy, forbye. She'd be working, but she had given him the car-phone number for an emergency. He'd never had a car and he'd sold the bike when Susan was born. No. She could wait. A remarkable recovery's not an emergency, after all. He'd had to cope on his own all through and he didn't need her now. On the last visit all she'd done was sit by Susan's bed saying, "Mummy's here! Open your eyes for Mummy!"

She had the cheek to say, "Didn't you see something was wrong?"

He'd lost his temper. "Ye cannae see a blood-clot, ye daft bitch! Whit d'ye think Ah've got? X-ray bloody specs?"

He'd been about to slap her when the nurse came in, raging, and sent them home. He looked at the clock and realised that he'd better get going to catch the shops open. He put on his jacket at the door, made sure he had some money in his pockets, and left. Running down the stairs he brushed the railings with his hand like a kid. In the close he shouted, "Ya beautyyy!" and savoured the echo. Out in the street he took his bearings for a moment before running up to the bakers on the corner.

He looked in the window. There was no bread left and only a few wee cakes and scones, so he didn't go right in. Instead he called out to the girl from the doorway, "Have ye a chocolate cake, love?"

"Naw." She didn't look up from her paper.

Never mind, he thought. There was another one up the road a bit. He ran on, over a crossing without looking. A car beeped loudly after him. At the bakery window he peered through the glass but couldn't see any cakes. It was a bigger shop, with brown bread and real cream cakes. The posh bakers, Susan called it. He went in and asked for a chocolate cake.

"Have you ordered one?"

The woman's voice was certainly not local. West End, probably.

"Naw. Ah'm no wantin' anythin' fancy, like. Jist a chocolate cake."

"You'll need to order one. It takes about two days. What's your name?" She took a little notebook from under the counter.

"Two days! Jesus Christ! Ma lassie's in hospital. She's jist woke up oot a bloody coma. She cannae wait two days fur a piece o' bloody cake."

The woman was speechless with disgust. Another, dressed identically, came in from the back shop to see the commotion. Alex stared dumbly at them, then fled.

There was a taxi outside, stopped at traffic lights. Alex jumped in. The driver thought he knew a shop that would have a cake – not far from the hospital, either. Alex relaxed. When they got there they had a chocolate cake, sure enough. It said 'Happy Birthday' in white icing and had a picture of a pussy-cat. It was three months to Susan's birthday, but it was all they had. Still, it would be like a birthday: they could have a wee party beside her bed.

He cradled the cake-box in his arms all the way to the hospital. In the lift he protected it like a baby from the crush. As he got nearer to the ward he wondered just how much better Susan was. It sounded like she was fine – as good as new. He wasn't surprised anymore. Why shouldn't it go as quickly as it came? Until she collapsed she was so cheery and bright. No-one could have guessed, not even Nancy.

There was a nurse standing at the door of the ward. He smiled and held up the cake-box for her to see. She obviously didn't know about Susan asking for it, because she looked puzzled. She opened a side door and showed him a room with arm-chairs and a coffeetable. There were copies of "Woman's Realm" and "Autocar".

"Can you wait in here, Mr Macleod?"

"OK," said Alex, warily. "Is everything aaright?"

"The Registrar will see you. In a minute. He's just coming."

"Can Ah no see Susie yet?"

But she'd already closed the door and was gone.

Sure everything was all right. She was probably smartening herself up. She always liked to be smart for Daddy. That made looking after her on his own a lot easier. Then again, maybe she wasn't entirely better. Anything was a remarkable improvement on a coma, after all. Maybe he'd expected too much. They were thoughtful about these things in hospital – they had to be. Nancy had burst into tears at the sight of all the tubes and wires.

The doctor came in, carrying a clipboard, and looked Alex up and down. "Mr Macleod."

It wasn't a question, but he paused as if waiting for an answer.

"Hello doctor. Ah brought the cake, like ye said on the phone, remember? By the way, Ah'm sorry Ah swore at ye. Ah wis …"

"Mr Macleod." He still paused. "Susan won't be having any cake."

Alex was about to interrupt but the doctor raised his hand and silenced him. "There was a setback. The improvement couldn't be sustained. She was too weak. It all happened very suddenly."

"Whit happened? Whit are ye sayin? Is she in a coma again?"

"No, Mr Macleod. I'm very sorry, but Susan died about half an hour ago. We tried to call you, but you had already left."

"Ah wis buyin the cake." Alex was quiet for a moment, then looked straight at the doctor's eyes, puzzled and hurt.

"You said she wis better."

"I said there had been a remarkable improvement. It was only the calm before the storm, as it turned out."

Alex stood up, uncomfortably close to the doctor who stepped back, bumping the coffee table. "You said she wis better! You said she wis better and wanted a chocolate cake. Ah brought the bloody cake!"

He thrust the box at the stomach of the white coat, no longer looking at the doctor's face. The doctor tried to push it back but Alex held fast. The clipboard became a useful barrier between them and the doctor consulted it closely. "You are RC aren't you? Yes. I've asked the priest to come to see you. He'll be here soon. Would you like a nurse to sit with you until then?"

Alex sat down again and started to sob, rocking back and forward with the cake-box in his arms.

"Whaur is she? Can Ah see her?"

"We're doing some tests. She will be in the mortuary after. There is a room there where you can see her later, if you wish."

"Doin' tests?!"

Alex was half-shouting, half-sobbing, looking up wildly at the doctor who retreated towards the door.

"Ye mean cuttin' her up? Could ye no wait? Did ye need the bloody bed that quick?!"

"We have to know what went wrong. They're only X-rays."

Alex was on his feet again. The doctor saw in his eyes a rage that was not there before. He signalled out of the door for a nurse to come. Alex was shouting at him from the other side of the room.

"She's hud millions of bloody X-rays. It's probably that that killed her!"

"I'll get a nurse, Mr Macleod. She can sit with you till the priest arrives."

Alex was suddenly and terribly calm. "Ah don't want a priest." He headed across the room towards the doctor. "Ah want to see Susan." He pushed past the flinching Registrar and out of the door. "Whaur's the mortuary?"

"Mr Macleod. You can't yet ..."

But Alex had gone, round the corner and into the lift. As the door shut behind him, he heard the doctor calling.

"Bastard!" said Alex.

He rode in the lift to the basement. The mortuary was probably there. He felt very calm now, though the cake-box was shaking in his hands. Out of the lift, he looked for a sign – there were red and green ones, long words he didn't recognise. He wondered how you spelt 'mortuary'.

He remembered he'd written to Susan's teacher to tell her the lassie was in hospital. He'd spelt coma as 'comma'. The teacher had come to see him and said it was a "good mistake". He should think of it like that: just a pause in Susan's life, not a fullstop. It was a full bloody stop now, though.

He looked through a glass door to see if he was in the right place. A nurse glared at him. He walked on more quickly and turned a corner. It was a dead end. He turned again and headed down the corridor. He was shaking more now and could feel the tears coming again. There were footsteps behind him. Without looking round, he ran up a nearby stairway and through the swing doors at the top, backwards, shielding the cake. He was in another corridor. All the signs were meaningless. A door opened nearby. He thought he heard his name called. In a panic, he opened the nearest door and slipped in.

He stopped for breath and tried to blink the tears from his eyes. Looking round he saw he was in the chapel. It was empty. On the altar a few candles flickered timidly before the crucifix. This is the last thing I need, he thought, and peered through the glass door to see if the corridor was clear to leave.

He was about to go when he noticed a notebook lying open on a table by the door. Beside it a printed card read 'Please enter here the name of anyone you wish to be remembered in our prayers.' He wondered, and took a closer look. The page was ruled in columns headed Name, Ward, Illness, Date. He looked down the page. There, at the bottom of the day's names was Susan Macleod, IC, Coma. He didn't recognise the handwriting.

He wondered if one of the candles had been lit for her. That would be just like the thing: the candle burning even after she was dead. He went up to the altar and watched them, the wee flames shaking in his heavy breath. One had almost burned out – that would be hers. He laughed weakly to himself, shaking his head, then looked up at the wooden crucifix. The cross was smooth and polished – a nice piece of work, he thought – but the body hanging there was rough and twisted and knotted.

You certainly huv it aa yer own way, he thought. Anythin good happens an' we're supposed tae thank ye on wur knees. Anythin bad an it's no your fault. Well ma Susan never did anythin bad in her life nothin tae deserve this. A nice wee lassie: everybody said so. Naebody did her harm; naebody but you. You made blood-clots – no me, no anybody. You. You're tae blame an' ye cannae bloody hide from it. You put me through hell. OK, Ah'm nae good. Ah know that. But Susie? Whit did she ever do? She loved ye. She cam in from school wan day sayin, "Daddy, I love Jesus." She bloody prayed tae ye. We aa prayed tae ye tae save her. But you didn't care, did ye? Ah mean, if ye wanted to save her you could save her. Oh you let her get better, but. Jist enough tae ask fur Daddy an' a bit o cake. But ye couldnae let her hing on for me tae get there. How d'ye think she felt, dyin, an' her Daddy no there? Naebody she knows, jist dyin in an empty room. "WIS HAUF AN OOR TOO LONG TAE WAIT?"

He had shouted aloud in the end. He found he had crushed the cake-box in his hands. He opened the lid and scooped out the bashed sponge. If he'd not run about looking for one he might have got here in time. What a bastard!

He roared incoherently, in fury, and hurled the cake at the crucifix. It struck full in the face. Icing and chocolate sponge stuck to the thorns. Cream filling smeared the cheeks and nose. Lumps of cake fell to the altar. He threw the box after it and then rushed back up the aisle, desperate to get out.

The priest and a nurse were standing in the chapel, the door still swinging behind them. "That's him," said the nurse, nervously.

The priest's voice was quiet, but ill at ease. "Mr Macleod? I've just heard about Susan. I'm very ..."

Alex barged past him, avoiding his eyes, and into the corridor. The nurse caught her breath. "Father, look at the cross! Look what he's done!"

"Never mind that," said the priest impatiently. "That's what it's for."

He followed Alex out into the corridor. Alex was stopping at every door, peering through the glass, muttering "Susie ... Susie ... Susie ..."

Donald Munro

illustration by Marlena Sielewicz-Stanhope

Harvey Holton

For Ilka Day

Cry cuckold the muin
they horns are nae mine
they pierce nae the herts
that milk white dreep slaw
oan the crammasy snaw;
They pierce nae the herts
that the hell-hoonds hairri.
The hunts noo whaur the geese hing,
early nicht whaun the licht maitters,
whaur the bulls horn the kist craters;
nae Eagle-daith the herts rip
nae bluid fued sterts or ends noo.

> For ilka day
> five items o knawledge
> frae awe wiselike fowk:
> the day o the sin's month
> the ages o the muin
> the sea-tide athoot error
> the day o the week.

Lang the day oan the yirds ruits,
lang the waitin oan lifes edge
rune readin yer ain lifes pledge.
Muckle the stick Deep Feeder
tap ruit sookin the centre
seekin the space whaur knawledge is born.
Atween beech brenches oan a winters nicht
the deep lift blinters its ain licht;
clear the bare stick staunds inset wie sternies
roond as the harns is the shape o the croon.
Subtle as nerve ends the sternies are pulsein
branches are beekit wie livein thocht.

> For ilka day
> ain item o knawledge
> frae awe wiselike fowk.

Its for man, if ony, tae say ocht
aboot the crazy pooer o a bluidlettin,
the crazy pooer o a wild creation
that begets poems an no bairns.
A hole it leaves in the faither's soul;
the hert wuid, sair centre, foul,
saes he is noo disjaskit, incompleat;
whummelt as a warrior.
Noo its his ain weird he maun dree
makin wie his ain mind an haund
patterns, messages oan wund an saund
wie nae mithers bluid in their banes.

> For ilka day
> twae items o knawledge
> frae awe wiselike fowk:
> the time o the bluidlettin
> the time o the begettin.

A boon the bluidlettin o weemin,
tae them the final act o creation.
Eftar derk nurture an growth a life
is giein in awe the stramash, the strife,
the clanjamfrie o the yirds quiet turnin.
Lunar puu oan tide an harns
seed an egg their fine daunce mak
wame enfoldit hert throb bricht
crammasy an ticht the licht.
Whaur life sterts creation begins
pentit in caves or hingin oan waas
sherp the blinter o the auld bluid.

> For ilka day
> thrice the items o knawledge
> frae awe wiselike fowk:
> the time o the egg
> the time o the seed
> the ages o the bluid

Brek yet the watters whaur the seeds blossom,
howl yet the lungs wie a crack that's awesome
as air breenges in expandin an fawin
catcht bi the beat o the hert new thumpin
airms an shanks get their first streetchin
fists baw an curl taes spier eftar walkin
word chords streetcht ticht harns bellow for talkin.
Noo seed an egg jine in jizzen bed
giein age again tae bluid borne patterns
that flow through bairn an timeless clans
haudin thegither wie a fierce fiery faith
the jowkin, jinkin, journey intill daith.

> For ilka day
> fower items o knawledge
> frae awe wiselike fowk:
> the seed o life
> the egg o life
> the time o birth
> the time o daith.

Breengein frae the belly button, the foreheid,
neck bent back oan saft skin liein
lips touch gowd an smeddum faws apairt
intae awe its mixter maxter bits; a lost clutch:
the snake swallies its tail, the torques ends touch.
In the spirelin circle the cumulus brek
an the pinnacle o the yird is lowssed,
baists real an ghaistlike trauchle owre the lift
the deid an undeid tak their shiftin seats
shank bane trumpets blaw the final beats
bodhrans crash, licht, pulse an fade
in ancient rhythms the yird is remade.

> For ilka day
> the fifth item o knawledge
> frae awe wiselike fowk:
> tae ken the hail sang athoot error.

Harvey Holton

Simon Darragh

What we can't say we can't say, and we can't whistle it either. (F Ramsey)

Beyond the last settlement, something went wrong.
That is to say, things started to misbehave.
No, not quite that. But, for instance, when I tried to shave,
I gazed, unfocussed, in the mirror, hours long.
Or someone would go for water, and not come back:
we'd find him paddling, or sitting on a rock.
The spanner would slip when one tried to change a wheel,
or the pencil-point snap when making notes. The feel
of everyday instruments was suddenly strange. Our guides
were useless: "It's always like that here," they said;
"We couldn't warn you; the only thing we know
is that, beyond this point, the radio fades,
and then we're on our own. The track led
a different way last year. Each time we go,
a new confusion takes us. Only later
it seems to us that something was gained: we falter
toward the idea that this time we got further,
yet have no certain record we can alter."

The Pathetic Fallacy

It comforts us to say "The angels watch,
send storms and comets on the Ides of March,
set a star to show that Christ is born;
the sun's eclipse; the temple curtain torn."

But the rejected lover
sees clearly in his despair,
as he leaves his love's last meeting,
and goes out, to discover
the heartless sun still beating
through the bland indifferent air.

He sees the fall of Icarus, the end
unnoticed by ship or ploughman. We pretend,
magnify mythology, to find
some meaning in the ripple left behind.

Caterpillar Poem

The caterpillar gasps to see
overhead, the butterfly:
"Unnatural! You won't catch me
up in one of them; I'd die!"

But Nature has so ordered things
that, earthbound, he must pass through dying,
wake again equipped with wings,
and, naturally, end up flying.

Holy Sonnet

Swedenborg, at dinner, calmly told
how he'd discussed the question with Saint Paul,
and Blake's sun was a chariot of gold
where others saw a sovereign-sized red ball.
These took their gifts for granted; knew that all
their fellow creatures had the power to hold
communion with the angels; for they fall,
men and angels, from the self-same mould.
In city centres now this power is sold
by clergymen and gurus with the gall
to foist on fashion's fools as new the old
half-lie, half-truth that God comes when we call.
One simple secret none of them can sell:
the faith of William or Emanuel.

Simon Darragh

Alison Prince

Weaving

Behind his prick-sharp shuttle, paying out,
The male thread shoots across the great abyss,
Creating new-made fabric with his kiss
And his departure. He can feel no doubt
That he progresses. He is moving on,
Achieving his ambitions, going far.
He does not look behind, lest it should mar
His onward movement. He is here and gone,
Engaged in making, not in what is made.

The warp strands part for him, then close behind
His substance, smoothly, so that he will find
No obstacle. His wishes are obeyed;
And yet he is between, and not above,
The female threads which bear his passing love.

A Shred

Once the belief in human good has gone
There can be no more faith in politics.
When passion dies, it leaves the empty tricks
Revealed, the greed stripped bare. The face that shone
With fervour is historic now, a ghost
Of simple trust in coming better days.
That innocence, that unselfconscious gaze,
Belongs in archive racks of Picture Post.
When cynicism rules, we dwindle through
The endless layers of doubt, and touch no ground
And wonder if belief can still be found
In anything. The barest shred is true;
That there is comfort in the sky's embrace
And in rain's kisses on the upturned face.

Fly

Carefully
Bring thumb and fingers to the fly
Which buzzes on the glass.
After the winter's sleep
She is confused,
As flustered as a big, fussed woman
Who has lost her bus pass.
She frets in my fingers,
Fizzing but not surprised.
Nothing could be more strange
Than the hard sky with its shut-out sun.
Take her to the door
And let her go.

Alison Prince

REVIEWS

Glasgow - One Party State?

Phantom Village: the Myth of the New Glasgow, Ian Spring, Polygon, £8.95; *Scotland at the Crossroads*, ed James D Young, £3.95; *Glasgow Limbo*, Jack Withers, £3.45; *The Last Threads: Life in a Glasgow Weaving Mill*, Ann Kerr, £2.45; *The Reckoning (Workers City)*, ed Farquhar McLay, £3.95, all Clydeside Press.

Determinations is an ambitious project by Polygon who seek, by publishing this series, to promote a debate within Scotland about our culture and "raise international issues which already affect Scottish experiences". Ambition indeed in a society which prides itself on its apparent disdain for its own history and culture. Ian Spring's book *Phantom Village: The Myth of the New Glasgow* is a determined attempt to address the paradoxes and contradictions currently prevalent in Glasgow and by so doing help us to understand something about the great changes taking place in that city. To do this he has taken a huge canvas upon which he attempts to locate much of the history of the city up until the present time, but while he is doing this, he also invokes and quotes from much of the literature associated with the city. At another level the book is also a moving, personal, leave-taking of the city. He is particularly good when dealing with Alasdair Gray's *Lanark*. He seems to have a particular insight into the physical environment from which Alasdair Gray's vision has sprung. He is also good on what could be described as the "verbal" aspects of some recent painting produced in Glasgow. Curiously, however, when developing his ideas about the narrative content of these works he omits altogether any consideration of the formal or stylistic means of communication. What is *being* communicated surely has a great deal to do with *how* it is being said.

Scotland at the Crossroads, unlike *Phantom Village*, does not seek to take a dispassionate overview. Its subtitle 'a socialist answer' says it all. This is a committed book, and that is its strength: Socialism is the answer to all Scotland's problems. After a decade of Thatcherism it is a brave person who would gainsay this verdict, but Glasgow is effectively a one-party, one-Lally, "Socialist" state. James D Young, as editor of *Scotland at the Crossroads*, takes 32 pages to define the socialist position on Scotland's future. One worries, however, about the veracity of the scholarship when we are told, on page 26, that Evelyn Waugh (*sic*) was abusive to the residents of Merseyside after the Heysel tragedy! The heart of this book is the re-printing of William McIlvanney's speech to the SNP conference in 1987, 'Stands Scotland Where It Did?'. In the short space of 11 pages he produces a stunning, humbling yet proud definition of what it means to be a Scot living in Scotland, while at the same time recognising the mortal dangers which face our culture. This is an historic statement.

There are other good, if anger-making, things in this book – Margaret Stewart's revelations about women being routinely humiliated in Corntonvale Prison by strip-searching (in 1985, when the average prison population was 174, 4219 such searches were carried out); and Helen Allen's family testimony relating to the shame felt in her family through generations arising from the eviction of her grandmother after the death of her grandfather who was gassed while serving in the First World War.

Helen Allen's anger is echoed in Jack Withers' *Glasgow Limbo*. To some it may seem an odd way to put it, but this depressing, depressive and angry book is also uplifting. The courage of the man is both amazing and humbling. Such is his hunger for expression that he can take subject-matter which seems unendurable and by his strength, art and humour give it form.

Ann Kerr's play, *The Last Threads*, is generally less black than *Glasgow Limbo* although its anger is vivid and real. The action takes place during the last hours of a Bridgeton thread mill and graphically describes the impact of multinational corporate decisions upon working people, their culture, and their sense of identity. At a political level this could be seen as a case history of the implications of allowing our society to become a satellite economy.

Glasgow is currently in the grip of an administration which is promoting the "Heritage Culture" and the "Art Industry" with single-minded determination. It is on record as saying that it will "milk" the latter for every penny it can get. Even people in other parts of Scotland seem to have been seduced by the glitter and false glamour of it all, but for those of us who live and work in Glasgow the reality of the situation is very different. Repression, censorship and suppression are rife. It is against this background that the group known as Workers City has emerged. They are a loosely-knit group of artists and intellectuals who are now providing the only sustained and serious opposition to the very powerful interests now seeking to subvert the artistic and intellectual life of Glasgow for their own ends. They are obliged to fight what is effectively a political battle for the soul of Glasgow since there is no other effective opposition. Some of the central issues which stand out from *The Reckoning*, their second book, are:

> **Farquhar McLay** – We are moving towards permanent non-employment of "workers" on a massive scale. The great year of culture has more to do with power politics than culture, more to do with millionaire developers than art.

> **Jack Withers** – Glasgow:
> Creative creatures here are nothing more than mere clowns
> at the consumer court of capitalism.

As Jack Withers implies, this is a determined effort by artists in Glasgow who are attempting to use their art to defend a culture. Their fight is not just about Glasgow or even about art. It is fundamentally about what kind of society we want to live in and to bequeath to our children.

All these books are essential reading for those seeking to brief themselves on the condition of Scottish culture at this time.

Ian McCulloch

The Temptation of Faust (Woodcut, 1988) by Ian McCulloch

Stories to Rede...

The Magic Flute, Alan Spence, Canongate, £12.95; *The Truth of Stone*, David MacKenzie, Mainstream, £12.99; *Poverty Castle*, Robin Jenkins, Balnain Books, £7.95.

Alan Spence's first novel is an ambitious one, covering 20 years in the lives of four boys from the southside of Glasgow. Set during the 1960s and '70s, the questing spirit of that time forms the novel's motor force. Spence's four are the same age, and from the same side of the religious track, first introduced as friends about to leave primary school. The recurrent symbol of the quest, the eponymous magic flute, is introduced in the opening scene when they go to enlist for the Orange band. Artistic Tam has the touch and the support of his parents, mental Eddie hasn't but is a dab hand at battering things with drumsticks, studious Brian wants to learn to play but is forbidden by his mother, while dull George does as his Masonic pater instructs and persists: he knows not why.

Though the Orange band is soon left behind, what follows is prefigured in this first scene: the boys remain the product of their home environments as first witnessed. Tam sets off, flute in hand, on the hippy trail with little opposition from the parental hearth; Brian continues with useful learning, Eddie becomes a gangster in short trousers, then joins up when things start to go wrong, while George plods on, into the world of Masonic orthodoxy which his father designs for him. Around Tam an array of period wierdos gather. Spence is good on the eclectic mishmash of druggy ideas current in this group. Yet he possesses such facility for storytelling that there is a danger of his slipping into the facile, as the fast-paced narration tends to treat the intense and the relaxed in the same easy tone, while the scale of the project means that much of the action is simply related at a distance, in a paragraph or two. It is his talent for dialogue which carries the reader through. Though their ideals prove time-bound, George, Tam and Brian survive. Eddie and John Lennon do not. The book ends with its

tail in its mouth, when Brian, having given up teaching, sends a story he has written about that first day at the Orange band to Tam.

Throughout his novel, Alan Spence quotes from and name drops the hip of the era liberally. Baby-boomer readers who share Spence's knowledge of the period will be enchanted by *The Magic Flute*, spurred to the attic to dust the Mahavishnu albums and the Alan Watts books wistfully. If the novel fails to satisfy, it may be because he treats this radical period in the contemporary manner, as an historical experiment which failed other than to manufacture a new set of marketing opportunities. The truth is more complex than that.

The Truth of Stone raises questions that don't surface in *The Magic Flute*. David S MacKenzie's first novel is a complex of different narratives from differing viewpoints, held together by the obsession of one James Atherton with Elsie McKillop, a young woman in her twenties who had disappeared, presumed dead, from a north-of-Scotland village, to reappear as the corpse of a 60-year-old woman in a local loch. Atherton reconstructs Elsie's life twice, giving the local view via an iconic series of photographs, and secondly through the investigations of a reporter from the *Ardallt Journal*, who trails her to Naples, where she lives as Elisa Stasi.

Where Spence's novel is clear to the point of transparency at times, MacKenzie relies on the relativity of truth to intrigue the reader. Versions of the story cancel out each other's claims to verity, leaving the reader guessing as to the actual events. If Spence's work is the full realisation of an older approach to the novel, in which the function of the writer is simply given as that of social documentarian, MacKenzie's is an incomplete attempt on a more challenging aesthetic, in which the writer's impulse to writing is the real mystery. *The Truth of Stone* promises much more from a writer aware of post-modern methods, hampered only by an inflexibly formal tone which does not take account of shifts in viewpoint. Yet this disclaimer is excused within the novel structure, which means that any criticisms of technique must be levelled at Atherton, and not MacKenzie.

The narrowness of highland life contrasts with the largesse of Neapolitan experience.

Elsie, like the reporter (and perhaps Atherton too), is the outsider who cannot belong in the narrow, yet finds no place in the broad. Her ultimate return, and fulfilment of that long-assumed fate as corpse in the loch, to suggests that underlying the absolute uncertainty of relativism, there is something more fundamental, an inescapable destiny.

Poverty Castle is also a book concerned with the business of writing, though its protagonist is not merely researching times past like Atherton, but attempting some kind of transcendence of the present by means of the writing of fiction. Born in 1912, Robin Jenkins continues to produce novels beyond the point when many contemporaries have retired into memoirs. Perhaps some critics would wish his activity to stop so that its achievement can be measured. Yet his creativity shows no sign of abating and perhaps there is something telling in the struggle of this, his fictional novelist, who wants to affirm essential goodness, to explain Jenkins' ongoing activity. His work over almost forty years has contained much of the dark side of human nature. *Poverty Castle*, while dipping into the shade, ends in the light.

In the first part of the novel, the Sempill family establish themselves in a mansion by the sea in Argyll, having rescued it from neglect. The five sisters are blessed with beauty, and the privilege they enjoy conspires to create something approximating to a paradisiacal existence. It is when the youngest of them, Diana, leaves to attend university in Glasgow that their good fortune is made most obvious, through the figure of Diana's room-mate, Peggy Gilchrist, whose background is sharply converse to Diana's. Poverty, and prejudice, brings us back into familiar Jenkinsland, yet here among the young and bright, there is at least the hope of change, there is a future worthy of a struggle towards levelling. If the older Sempills endure a sense of loss, with all its attendant loneliness, the young do not succumb. Ultimately, it seems that the impulse towards an ideal, whether in reality or in fiction, is a constant, known as hope. As long as that can be sustained, the spirit will remain creative. **Robert Alan Jamieson**

Rough Diamonds and Cultured Pearls: New Poetry

The Gangan Fuit, Ellie McDonald, Chapman, £4.95; *Leonard's Shorter Catechism*, Tom Leonard, AK Press, £1.95; *This Folding Map*, Alan Riach, Auckland University Press, no price; *Ridings Writings/Scottish Gothic*, Chris Bendon, Stride, £4.50. *Pierrot*, Harry Smart, Faber & Faber, £4.99; *Sting*, George Gunn, Chapman, £5.95.

Included here are two collections in the *Chapman* New Writing Series. Ellie McDonald's *The Gangan Fuit*, and George Gunn's *Sting*. *The Gangan Fuit* is "dedicated to the lover of words" and it is evident from her poems that this poet has a deep feeling for and strong relationship with, her language. Her Scots is not sentimental, but robust and vital. In *The Gangan Fuit* Ellie McDonald sets out her poetic and cultural beliefs and concerns in poems like 'Halloween', a warning cry but not yet a lament for her threatened language of Scots, and 'Limbo' "Hae ye seen yon words o mine/ on yer traivels?/ I gied them awaa,/ an ilka ain sae dear./ They maun be ettlan/ tae be hame nou,/ my puir wee hurtit bairnies./ Wad ye ken them whan they spak?" Disjecta membra or palinode?

McDonald is also concerned with developing the Scots lyric tradition, evidenced by the high proportion of songs and short lyric pieces in the collection, 'Sang O Joy', 'Luv Sangs' or 'Outness'. Versatile and diverse, she also includes two turnings from the Suddron of Wm Shakespeare: the existential Soliloquy from Act 2 Scene 2 of *Hamlet*, and Act 3 Scene 1 from *A Midsummer Night's Dream*. There is some work of her own in the Suddron tongue, but her Scots is the more successful.

Tom Leonard's *Shorter Catechism* is a series of Questions and Answers not on the theme of "Who made me?" but on the enormities of the deliberate genocide waged in the Middle East, preceded by an essay 'On the Mass Bombing of Iraq and Kuwait, Commonly Known As "the Gulf War."' It is difficult to approach critically a work of this kind – according to Adorno there could be no more poetry after Auschwitz. Yet, one of the functions of poetry is to make us think. This work reflects on the hypocrisy of the many parties involved. Our own politicians emerge from the debate as neither noble nor principled.

Chris Bendon's *Ridings Writings/ Scottish Gothic*, his second book, is a curious two-part collection on Northern themes. The first is a sequence on the Ridings of Yorkshire, a contemplation, a quiet celebration, a song of himself in many ways. The second part consists of 16 quietly impressive snap-shot poems on Scottish themes with echoes of MacDiarmid heard in 'Stoned'.

From another Yorkshireman comes *Pierrot*, Harry Smart's first collection. Confident, precise writing, but I found difficulty in making the poems work for me.. With the exception of the haunting irony and terror of 'Dante at Birkenau' where "the inferno is not a place beyond control,/ here, withal, doth Christ's writ run", they did not move or excite me.

Alan Riach's *This Folding Map* contains very fine pieces. The book is prefaced by a charming and witty 'Memo' and closes metaphysically on the unfixedness of one's native land and the journeys that are made through it. The poems take nature, landscape, people, love, and Riach's native Lanarkshire as their subjects. 'The Heron' displays a similar kind of delight for language and artifice found in MacCaig's poetry: "To you who are long gone/ and far away/ I send/ these words, rolling down and round the world./ For answer/ you'll send midnight to me from your distant place/ and I'll return it./ And nothing more will ebb away." 'MacDiarmid's Language' is an expression of Riach's particular sympathy for CMG's work, and abounds in epiphanies where metaphors assume a magic realism. Lyrical, elegiac, gnomic, ironic, his poems are confident. A good first collection.

The other title in *Chapman*'s New Writing Series is *Sting* by George Gunn. This work will, I am sure, establish Gunn's place in the mainstream of contemporary Scottish writing. With several pamphlets of poems already published, his first book is a set of well-made poems that sing amidst the uncertainty of the late twentieth century. This book distinguishes itself from the others above in the sheer force of its passion. The collection is in

many ways a journey from "the strath/ of deer & eagle/ of salmon and & cat" to the horrors of the city, exemplified in the poem 'Glaschu', "a huddled gaff of destitutes/ whacked & rammied into/ cortina bricks hugging like a shadow/ over a pissed-full puddle/ of Gaelic evictions". A journey out of Eden.

The best of his writing is found in the opening poem 'The Box', a long poem which allows us to see the extent of his craft and the full force of his voice. 'The Box' is part elegy and part un-quiet meditation on the state of Scotland and the position of the Celt. A moving piece, it is rich in images and intricate in its development of the ballad measure which shows this form is still capable of carrying great poetry. The influence of the work of Sorley MacLean is evident here: I think particularly of 'Hallaig' and 'Elegy for Calum I MacLean'. But acts of poetic homage do not lessen the worth of any work, they increase it. Other poems shine out equally strongly, especially those *in memoriam* Jan Palach, Lorca, Connolly, Morris Blythman; and the 'Liberty Ode' for Hamish Henderson, happily still with us, who "writes Scotland's name large/ upon the page of the world" and who, like Swift, serves human liberty. **Michael Lister**

Mair Scottish Fiction

A Den of Foxes Stuart Hood, Methuen, £13.99; *Mother Glasgow*, John Burrowes, £9.99; *A Quiet Stranger*, Robbie Kydd, £14.99, both Mainstream.

I found Stuart Hood's new novel difficult to begin with. It seemed to be Science Fiction, and I can't bear SF. In fact, it's complicated, but it's not SF at all. The SF parts are introduced to show that no matter how the world progresses and how far people travel to and settle on new planets, Fascism will always be there with its victimisation of women, its relentless puritanism and its campaign of extermination against anyone who deviates in any way from what Fascists regard as "normal."

Peter Sinclair, a retired left-wing academic, rents an isolated cottage on a conservative major's Highland estate. Peter's ruminations about his past and present are interrupted by a letter from Christopher Williams, who lives at La Volpaia (Den of Foxes) near Siena, asking him to take part in a "wargame" about Andromeda, a planet inhabited by the Pilgrim Fathers from Earth in the year 2087. He agrees, partly from boredom, partly because of his wartime memories of fighting with partisans against both Mussolini and Hitler in that part of Italy.

Peter's wargame starts with an account of the lives of David Balfour and his girlfriend Catriona, both space-scouts and electronics engineers for the Pilgrim Fathers, who spy on all their workers and are quick to exterminate anybody suspected of not adhering to the colony's strict regime . The Control Commission believes Andromeda is about to be invaded from Planet Earth, so the spying is intensified, and a young woman Isabel Dufy is extruded, otherwise put to death by imprisonment in a capsule and shot into space. David is worried because Isabel and Catriona were friends, and he wonders if Catriona will do anything to make the Pilgrim Fathers suspect that she disagrees with their astringent regime.

The major's young relative, Lucy, in leather gear and riding a motor-bike, arrives and Peter falls in love with her, though she is less than half his age. They become lovers, and this causes tension between the major and Peter, especially as the major, an old widower, has his own eye on Lucy and tries unsuccessfully to get her to mount him like a horse or a motor- bike. The affair doesn't last long. Lucy leaves for an unknown destination, and Peter goes to see Christopher Williams in Italy.

Peter revisits the scenes of his wartime exploits and searches for the grave of a young German whom he and a partisan had killed. Lucy turns up at La Volpaia and asks Peter to take photographs of an Israeli yacht which, she says, contains terrorists plotting against the Palistinians. He does so, remembering that his own son by his former Israeli wife, may be one of the terrorists. Peter returns to Scotland, to the major's cottage and resumes his writing about the wargame, although he has got tired of it.

He describes the love between David and Catriona being shattered when Catriona is suspected of being lesbian. Catriona is put in a space-capsule and extruded. The victimisation of women is shown again when Peter finds the body of Miss Grizelle, the major's sister, a harmless old woman who minds her own business. She has committed suicide after being subjugated all her life by the major and his Polish overseer.

The plot is complicated, but the purpose of the novel is not.. Hood does not believe that life on a new planet will be any better than it is now and that tyranny with its secret agents and hidden microphones will flourish and destroy everyone suspected of deviation. I agree. That's why, overcoming the difficulties caused by several plots, I read it with great enjoyment. And I'll look forward to re-reading it soon, now that I know its theme.

Mother Glasgow, the third volume of John Burrowes's trilogy about the Gorbals, might be accused of having a hand in the victimisation of women, seeing that the heroine, Star Nelson, disappears from the narrative for exceedingly long periods at a time. Mind you, John Burrowes, unlike some male writers, does not show women as the despised weaker sex, for the plot arises out of Star's plan for vengeance on the villain who has murdered her father, a plan that miscarries and leads to one of the horrible murders in the book, so here women characters are given equal status with men; and indeed the minor women characters are well drawn. But the book is about gang warfare in Glasgow, the machinations of the Mafia in New York, the trouble caused by teenage larrikans in Australia, and IRA bombing in a Glasgow suburb; so its is definitely intended to be machismo.

The chief characters are Star's uncle, Sammy Nelson, and gangster Sonny Riley, who gets help from a member of the IRA, with subsequent horrific bombings. It is a good story, but it would have been a lot better if it had been tightened up and some great wads of unnecessary narrative taken out. For instance, seventy pages in the first half are devoted to Sammy's meetings with old Gorbals pals in New York and his outwitting of the Mafia. All this may be interesting enough, but it holds up the central narrative, and I got thoroughly bored with it and was relieved when Sammy returned to Glasgow and got into the main action. In fact, what was needed was not a pruning knife but a hatchet. Does Mainstream not employ an editor who will hack ruthlessly at the author's side-steps that may interest himself but are not relevant to his main theme?

An editor was also needed to do a hatchet work on Robbie Kydd's historical novel about the Carribean island of Tobago in the latter half of the 18th century. Many of the incidents in *The Quiet Stranger* are trivial, and there is too much repetition. We don't need to be reminded so often about Dickie's weaknesses and his brotherly love for the slave-girl Betsy because her mother had suckled them both as babies? And there are too many scenes showing Dickie's tom-boyish horse loving sister Antoinette's desire to be top dog before she becomes the mad wife of Mr Rochester.

The hero Dickie, or Richard Mason, the quiet stranger from *Jane Eyre*, is described by Jean Rhys as "a sly man and he will tell you a lot of nancy stories, which is what we call lies here." I would not call Dickie a liar, but I found him a bore. He tells his story in pastiche eighteenth century writing, occasionally addressing "the dear reader", about his life in Tobago while it was still a British possession and then was taken over by the French during the revolution. It meanders on and on. Much as I like historical novels, I just could not get interested in Dickie's life dominated first by his fearsome Scottish father and mad Antoinette and then by his cloying love for Betsy.

Fred Urquhart

Present Enlightenment

St Nynia, John MacQueen, Polygon £7.95; *Ossian Revisited*, ed Howard Gaskill, Edinburgh University Press, £30; *Studies in the Philosophy of the Scottish Enlightenment* (Oxford Studies in the History of Philosophy vol 1) ed M A Stewart, OUP, £37.50; *The Scottish Enlightenment and other essays*, George Davie, Polygon, £5.95; *Virtue by Consensus*, Vincent Hope, OUP £20.

Nearly as much as Nynia, 'Ossian' Macpherson needs unwinding from knitted legend. As John MacQueen stresses (revising his definitive 1961 book) what little can be fairly believed about "St Ninian" emerges only after virtuoso criticism of innumerable interpreta-

tions of the written sources – with reference to the different peoples in different territories in 5th century Scotland, confusions from the Venerable Bede to the present day as to who and where the Picts, the Gall-Gaidhill &c were; and the sundry patterns of hagiography, allegorisation and quasi-biography. The story-of-the-story of Nynia is itself a rich cultural history, the monastic terseness of MacQueen's prose achieving rare clarity with maximum compression and an odd fascination. Winifred MacQueen's translations of two key documents are new to this edition.

In *Ossian Revisited* Donald Meek's account of the Gaelic ballad is magisterial: origins and development in relation to other genres, recorded and likely extent, relation to and of the legend of the poet Ossian/Oisean, and the legends of Finn & co sung in his name. As regards the story of James Macpherson, historian, cobbler together of the in-large-part-forged *Fingal*, &c, Howard Gaskill points to Dr Samuel Johnson, who in a brilliant piece of invective provided the basis for subsequent debate about Macpherson, and the autheniticity of his 'Ossianic' poems. English habits of sneering at Scotland had much to do with subsequent silences when the "forgery" nature of Macpherson's "epic" had become clear. David Hume practised a subsequent extraordinary and very uncomfortable diplomacy on the subject. Cross-border English snobbery was nasty at the time.

Johnson's demand for clear evidence can be dismissed. He knew nothing of what actual evidence there could be, and made demands for proof as unreasonable as that Oisean himself be asked. An Aberdeen pupil of Thomas Reid, Macpherson was no morally inane self-seeking fake. Some of his work afforded beginnings for Celtic studies which didn't develop quickly enough. Possibly influenced by Thos. Blackwell's account of Homer as compiler from ballads rather than original poet, his attempted construction of a 3rd century Celtic epic has to be seen in perspective.

Macpherson's 'epic' had appeal as poetry even to those who thought it fake but were unconcerned at that.. In its primitive character, no less its flattering picture of refined early-Gaelic manners, it fitted what was expected and hoped for. Yet the cult of feeling was a humanising, ethical movement, dated like a sermon by the mores of those it reformed. It was meant to move people, when they needed to be moved. That Macpherson had the collossal European impact he did,indicates a temporary because timeous character. When it appeared there was nothing like it., exploding habits of language and limitations of expression, spawning for instance Blake's Prophetic Books, and beside Adam Ferguson, Macpherson was a father of Romanticism.

Subsequent implications for Scotland remain worthy of more investigation, the stuff Gaels rightly recoil from. Even if Macpherson's poem could have been a genuine 3rd century epic it would have communicated no recent picture of the Gael. Yet through later twilightisms it still influences assumptions about the Gael. It also represents aspects of human feeling which still need looking at critically. Gaskill's is a valuable book, its extensive account of an 18th century Scottish background which gave birth to modern academic literary study has its own importance.

M A Stewart's book is also of real present import.. The project started with the planning of a new journal. It gives instructive evidence of the huge impact of new scientific thinking (Newton, Boyle &c) on a wide range of university-educated Scots, not just scientists. This early scientism had much to do with the subsequent establishment of social sciences which have not in all respects improved on their beginnings.

Roger Emerson errs, pooh-poohing accounts of Scottish Enlightenment thought as deriving from classical republican theory as worked out by Fletcher of Saltoun. Why, in following Fletcher's lead, could 18th century Scots not have got a great deal from intellectual models drawn from new work in the natural sciences – and vice versa? Influence is multiple and hardly "either-or" exclusive. Commendably Roger Emerson attacks the account of pre-1700 Scotland as "fallowminded, fertilised entirely by imports" given by Lord Dacre (aka Hugh Trevor Roper) with the same sureness to be found when he spoke on Macpherson, or declared the Hitler diaries genuine. Scotland pre-1720 was no *campus rasus* but scene of considerable intellectual activity. The ill-named Scottish Enlighten-

ment was contiguous with what preceded it, and, with more to feed on with other, changing intrinsic factors, the country took off.

John P Wright's account of physiology and philosophy in the Scottish 18th century delves deep into unpublished lectures by William Cullen et al, notably Robert Whytt, revealing real modern relevance in Whytt's early attempts to question Cartesian views of mind in the light of new physiology studies. Whytt's advanced criticisms are startlingly un-biological. Biological thinking came later and makes Whytt's formulations seem odd, but shows how acute were his experiments and observations, so advanced as to have organised thought on the relation between mind and neurophysiology in terms still able to clarify 20th century problems.

Whytt's teacher George Young is interesting, for Young was, with the notable George Turnbull, a member of the Rankenian society, an early 18th century Edinburgh student intellectual club whose importance George Davie explored in a pioneering 1965 article. Davie's account of the 1690s, debates with Fletcher and subsequent developments following the 1707 Union, does a great deal in his brief selection of essays to reveal the beginnings, nature and abiding importance of the Scottish 18th century enterprise in creation of Civil Society. The second essay in his new book, his 1973 Dow Lecture, is in sharp, measured criticism of a modern liberalist viewpoint exemplified by T C Smout's attack on older Scottish educational priorities.

Davie rejects the view that it is perfectly adequate to enact physical social reform, without thought of persisting in the higher education of at least some of the populace. The human mind is not such that it can be conditioned *later*, applying new mechanistic techniques, and producing a happy, egalitarian and individualist society, all problems solved. The psychology implicit in Smout's approach is not borne out by experience, and 1980s disesteem of education has a lot to do with such naturalist individualist theories. Smout conveniently ignores the fact that such predecessors of Davie's view as John Burnet were energetic workers for open education for all, if refusing to kill all other priorities.

They were also part of an intellectual culture whose fecundity and radical intellectual character is evidenced in Davie's essay on Robertson Smith, not merely the editor of *Encyclopaedia Britannica* dismissed from his theological professorship for "heresy", but an anthropologist of great importance through his influence on Freud. Not the least commendation of this essay is its vivid picture of Victorian Edinburgh's passionate intellectual life, but it is also a literary *tour de force* in its counterpointing of references while sustaining the great sweep of the story. Davie's other paper here appeared first as prologue to Arthur Thomson's biography of J F Ferrier, and indicates both the obscurity into which a major Scottish thinker has been let fall, and the crucial character of Ferrier's philosophy in working out mutual implications of later continental philosophy in terms of an earlier Scottish philosophy still in Ferrier's day neither off the curriculum nor obscure.

Scouting neglected detail of great importance, Stewart's book combines well with Davie's in revealing the still "Hidden Scotland" lost if also forgotten. Importantly the place of Francis Hutcheson as "father" of the Scottish Enlightenment is not distinct from his liberalism in politics, like that of his friend the sometime Rankenian George Turnbull at Aberdeen. One can see from Richard Sher that at Glasgow Hutcheson enjoyed public prestige as a teacher of morality, occasioning the envy that energised Edinburgh's city council to look for a comparably gifted Moral Philosophy professor (Adam Ferguson).

Virtue by Consensus sorts out the different, related perspectives on morality of Hutcheson, his pupil Adam Smith, and Hutcheson's critic David Hume: on the fact and nature of seeing oorsels as ithers see us, and seeing them by sympathy/empathy as we see oorsels; on the differential importance of self-interest and concern for different others, as factors both in the individual mind and in society. Dr Hope suggests that only those who achieve a kind of personhood, empathy, balance of interests, *deserve* the moral considerations which ought nonetheless not to be withheld: what *claim* is there? Without denying morality an objective character, it is a discovery produced by discussion between men, concerning their own responses and ob-

servations. The key notion is Virtue, and the virtue of Dr Hope's book is at the start in establishing the different perspectives of his 18th century authors, and at the end arguing a modern moral philosophy clearly demonstrating that his chosen authors belong by no means to the past.   **Robert Calder**

Three Great Literary Figures

Autobiographies, Kathleen Raine, £12.99; *Collected Journals 1936-42*, David Gascoyne, £10.99, both Skoob Books, *Teorie e Altre Liriche*, Peter Russell, Carlo Mancuso Editore, Via Domenico Berti 36, 00135 Roma, Italy.

Raine's three Autobiographies in one volume. Beautifully written, this account of her life is necessary background to this Scottish poet's unique tale of poems. I say Scottish, though this is little known in Scotland. Born just south of the border in Northumbria, Scotia irredenta, her mother's people came from Edinburgh: "From Scotland my people had come ... Scotland is to this day a matriarchal country, and my mother's family naturally regarded me as my mother's daughter rather than my father's ... from my mother's side I inherited ... the memories of Scotland in song, speech, and heroic story ... the poet in me is my mother's daughter, and owes more to that lost birthright than to all the extraneous book learning I have since acquired." She enlarges on this theme, and of the poetry in her mother and her Aunt Peggy, a school teacher.

The three books *Farewell Happy Fields*; *The Land Unknown*; and *The Lion's mouth*, trace her life from those idyllic days in Bavington, with the magic homeland just the other side of the Cheviots. through teen age in London; Cambridge University; two broken marriages; the spiritual-poetic intense friendship with her Scottish Northumbrian compatriot, writer Gavin Maxwell, to her long years domiciled (exiled?) in Chelsea. There she still lives,in her 84th year busy editing the book-length review *Temenos*, and running the Temenos Academy of Integral Studies. A life of seeking, suffering, in love with nature and her eternal world, the spiral of the seasons, her spiritual home in Wester Ross, and above all – though she says little of it – of hard and creative work all of which bears the stamp of her remarkable genius. The centre of a circle of friends large and various, she is a source of inspiration and generous encouragement to all lucky enough to share, in however small a way, the warmth of the creative imaginative life that breathes in these pages. Through these autobiographies, poems and works of scholarship a wide readership has been drawn into that circle of heat and light, and that circle will be widened by new readers through this story of a beautiful and unique spirit.

Younger readers of *Chapman* may not know as much of David Gascoyne as they might. Born in 1916, he was the youngest of an exceptionally gifted trio of poets a generation on from the Auden-Spender group: George Barker and Dylan Thomas being the other two. He is also associated with lifelong friend Kathleen Raine. As much at home in French as English literature, he was particularly interested in the French surrealists such as Andre Breton. His first book was published when he was sixteen, but it was mainly in the '40s that his work became widely known and accepted. He knew all that was being done in the surrealist movement and almost everybody who was doing it. These *Journals* form a background to the period before he achieved fame, mainly with the collection of his Poems published by Tambimuttu and Poetry London, illustrated by Graham Sutherland. Much of the journals involves people few readers will know, but shadows of the famous flit through as personal friends. He writes a brief but informative description, for instance, of Picasso's studio during one of his visits there. Written with fluency and precision pf style, these journals take us up to the beginning of a series of breakdowns which afflicted him for years, a season in hell from which he emerged triumphantly to marriage and his present serene life as a Grand Old Man of Letters. Apart from its intrinsic interest, this book is a source of the literary history of its times. It should be read in conjunction with the poems, poems of imaginative vision, deep social, spiritual concern, and rare commitment. I was so impressed, back in the 50s, by a Third Programme broadcast of a new long poem,

Night Thoughts, that I wrote to the BBC and asked for a copy of the script. I still think it a major poem, full of the intensity of vision which characterises the best of his work.

Born in 1921 in Bristol, Peter Russell left England in 1964 and has lived abroad ever since, mostly in Italy and Canada where he was professor of poetry. Therefore he has not had the recognition in this country his exceptional gifts and dedication should have earned him. In the 50s in London, among much other work, he ran the magazine *Nine*, one of the best poetry reviews of this century. He was a friend of Eliot and Pound, publishing an anthology of Pound's saws on poetry. He knew everybody then writing, and was admired by most, including MacDairmid, who rated him highly. His output is large, and the present book of *Teorie* (simply "musin(g)s": visions, prophecies, revelations, meditations) *e Altre Liriche*, is a hardback collection of some sixty lyrical poems in English with Italian translations, introduction and notes: a small group from his total output, published in 1990.

Most of the poems here are in simple ballad metre, strictly and carefully crafted. But only the form is simple. The content of the poems is as complex and intricate as one would expect from an erudite polyglot polymath, ranging through history and European literature with the ease of a native. They are full of intellectual struggle, emotional conflict, lyrical beauty, the sense of nature and creature life, spiritual and philosphical questions and the great mysteries. Perhaps the outstanding poem is the one celebrating his own marriage *'Epithalamium.'* This sustains a parallelling of arithmetic and philosophic thought which challenges comparison with the great "metaphysical" canzone of Cavalcante, *'Donna mi pregza'*. I don't fully understand it myself, but recommend readers new to Russell to begin with it and work out to the rest of the book from that. You will then be left wondering how much could be packed into the simple form of these poems so masterfully and, often, with such beauty. Now in the 72nd year of a heroic life of running at life and riding its punches, there can be no doubt this is one of the best poets of our time.

Tom Scott

Theatre Roundup

If the theatre-going public, that unquantifiable entity, was given the chance to select its own season of drama, what would it comprise? The question is pertinent since Scottish theatres, particularly reps, have been throwing their winter nets wider, and trawling deep in an attempt to haul in recession-bitten audiences. The consensus, at least in the East, seems to be that audiences want comedy, nostalgia and mild suspense: the theatrical equivalent of comfort-eating.

The gorging began in December with a glut of pantos. Every theatre stoked up with busloads and school-parties to see them through the lean months to come. The best shows of the bunch were both written by Scotland's fairytale prince, Stuart Paterson. His *Snow Queen*, revived by Neil Murray at Dundee Rep, was total enchantment, and at Edinburgh's Royal Lyceum his new play *Shinda the Magic Ape* muscled streetwise slapstick in amongst a planet-friendly moral and edge-of-the-seat adventure. *Shinda* deserves a secure future with the frequent revivals of Paterson's more traditional Christmas shows, but at a time of year when audiences demand a name they know, it is an unusually brave management that risks the unfamiliar.

Come January, the East coast was gulping down a consignment of comedy thrillers. *Arsenic and Old Lace* at the Lyceum, *Corpse!* at Dundee Rep, and *The Lady of Phillimore Walk* at Perth did the best business the theatres had seen in months. The response of anyone who likes their comedy to make them laugh can only be that if people want this stuff they should pay for it themselves and stop clogging up the arteries of the subsidised theatres.

A solitary orient pearl: in February the Lyceum's *The Marriage of Figaro* sparkled with uncharacteristically exuberant inventiveness, and choice casting made it a lucky-dip where every surprise turned out to be just what you'd always wanted. Anarchy held in check by good humour set the tone of a production blithely stage-managed by an adept and likeable Figaro and filled out by a host of superb comic performances. If such lightness and verve were guaranteed, one could stomach a great deal of this candy-floss, but the recipe for the Lyceum's Summer Season reads like a marsbar diet. Four comedies - Byrne, Wodehouse, Stoppard, Coward - are lined up as if for a pie-eating contest, and the rumour that the theatre dreams up its summer programme to satisfy demand from American tourists is the only theory that makes sense of this schedule.

Thankfully the West has had a healthier winter. At the sepulchral Arches Theatre, director Andy Arnold has gone a long way to fill the temporary void left while the Tron accommodates its new seating and the Traverse waits in frustrated limbo for its new building to be finished. Arnold has put together a season incorporating work by the Arches Theatre Company and from other Glasgow-based companies. The first of the latter was a revival of Manfred Karge's *Conquest of the South Pole*, a quirky, expressionist drama about human resilience in the face of such torments as Polar exploration and unemployment. Rain Dog Theatre Company weighed the play down to earth with heavy Glaswegian overtones and a deliberately aggressive atmosphere. The result emphasised the debilitating shackles of poverty and redundancy at the expense of the play's poetic aspirations, and added a furiously pessimistic coda in the form of a Bob Dylan rant. Not nice, not artistically rounded, but exhilarating.

The Arches' own production of Pinter's *The Caretaker* was more controlled, but no less effective. Stringently directed, yet retaining an edge of unpredictability, this performance made perfect sense of Pinter's tawdry tragedians, so that the infamous pauses, hesitations, catches, tongue-tied silences were as revealing as the words. When work of this calibre is being produced with minimal funding, it makes a nonsense of our big, expensive ideas of what theatre is. Arts Council funding policies would turn you to Bolshevism.

Another small, poor theatre, Cumbernauld, played a winning card with their home-grown production, *To*, by Jim Cartwright. As 7:84 discovered with his first play *Road*, the Bolton playwright's hard-nosed, soft-hearted North of England settings translate successfully into a Scots register. *To* is a two-hander which presents more than a dozen characters in the course of a night down the local pub. Blythe Duff and Vincent Friel showed their mettle in a virtuosic display of quick-change personae, and created just the right atmosphere, flickering between brittle comedy and small-scale anguish. Cartwright has been criticised for writing in short scenes: throwing dramatic darts rather than performing the careful exploratory surgery of classical playwrights. But his thumbail sketches build into a portrait of a society. He is a verbal Hogarth, and we ignore him at our peril.

Rumours of the demise of the Tramway seem to have been so much chaff, and as long as the performance arena pulls in such a rich haul of international theatre, no one is complaining. The Tramway gives a view of big theatre which has nothing to do with plush front-of-house, or waving to your friends in the Dress Circle. Here are touring productions which are expensive, yes, and highly subsidised, but which put that money into the people and materials which make extraordinary things happen on stage.. The highpoints of the past three months at the Tramway have been Theatre Repere's *The Dragon's Trilogy*, and the RSC's *Electra*. The *Trilogy* is a six-hour story with a soap-opera engine and a bottomless mine of theatrical imagery. It tells the tale of Canada: not the politics and the demographic trends, not the national costume and the GNP, but all the little lives, the individual joys and pains which add up to a truly democratic history and, ultimately, to the future.

Performed by a near-faultless ensemble, the production meandered through a representative family group, exploring the ties that bind and loosen, from Quebec during the Depression, through wartime in Toronto, and present-day Vancouver, throwing lines of blood and love back to China and Japan. Director Robert Lepage and his co-creators build a miraculous edifice of images, imagined truths and momentary significances, celebrating the millions of forgotten lives.

Similarly elemental, but significantly different in style, Deborah Warner's production of Sophocles' *Electra* arrived in Glasgow trailing glorious reviews, and sold out before the unwary could say Fiona Shaw. That particular actress, in the title role, was the focus for the play's lionisation in London, and understandably so. She gave a heartrending performance as a woman ruined by the need for revenge. Naked under a torn shift, splattering barefoot through water and across the unrelenting stone of the stage, she presents Electra like a specimen on a slide, horrifying, agonising, inescapably true. To single out Shaw, however, is to underestimate the cohesion and balance of Warner's production as a whole. From the first rattle of an exploratory pebble on the stage, to the final, tragic bewilderment of Electra, facing freedom like an animal bred in captivity, this is a vortex of a play that grabs audiences from behind their expectations and whirls them into its intense, engulfing drama.

Like an early Spring, just when everyone is rubbing financial chilblains and spreading their energies thin, the Citizens opens two new studio spaces and turns the theatre into a buzzing honeycomb of activity. Three new plays opened in as many days in February, and the excitement generated is the best thing to happen to Scottish theatre since the Havergal/Prowse/MacDonald phenomenon came up the Clyde. The new studios seat 70 and 130 people apiece, and have been created where the theatre's bars stood. Interval milling and swilling now take over the foyer, whose cool, clean, interior-designed look has been banished in favour of the black-and-gold glister of the main auditorium. The opening shows and forthcoming attractions are an intriguing mixture of the unknown and the unusual with a strong European flavour. A little-known Strindberg, a Botho Strauss, and Brecht's *Edward II* are a taste of things to come, and the present trio are a new translation of a Chilean play, the first stage production of Craig Raine's *"1953"*, and a new adaptation of P.G. Wodehouse's *Summer Lightning*.

All three shows had that edge of uniqueness and challenge which one almost takes for granted at the Citz, but misses so badly in other Scottish venues. Robert David MacDonald's translation of *Niagara*, a strange involving drama by Alonso Alegria, was like a walking manifesto. The suggestion that the right people with a strong enough commitment to their art and a belief in the apparently impossible can work miracles, matches the conviction that our theatre people need to fight off grey, clay-footed accountants busy with their balance-sheets and corporate hospitality, trussing up our widest dreams.

Craig Raine's update of Racine's *Andromaque*, was broadcast on Radio 3 in 1990, but only now makes its explosive stage debut. *"1953"* is a very clever play, feeding new blood and guts into Racine's statuesque but, to our ears, chilly text. Instead of the misty distances of Greek history, the action rears up out of a frighteningly convincing post-war Europe where Hitler holds sway and Britain is a tragic name from the past. Philip Prowse's white-hot production was a tactile expression of the play's pain and evil. It wrenched a superb performance from Greg Hicks, and showed without a shadow of a doubt that the studios at the Citizens are the spaces to watch.

Julie Morrice

Pamphleteer

A wounded raven, a rabid hound and Vincent van Gogh's dismembered ear make their symbolic presence felt in Wolfgang Bächer's *Doors of Smoke* (Statis, Malcolm Rutherford, 14 Greenhill Place, Edinburgh, EH10 4BR, £1). They inhabit poems primed with angst and philosophical grievance which seem just too careful, knowingly guised in a rural filmy sense of French existentialism gone thoughtfully awry that tends to negate any real emotional impact on the reader. More convincing are the poems of Urs Oberlin in *Flamingo Dance* (Statis, £1). Oberlin sticks to a less dramatic image than Bächer, and homes in on a little more humanity, gathering shards of truth and holding on to them. Echoes of death trace minimally in the poem *Crossing*, and tell us of "a man, violet-dark,/ you felt the touch of his cloak,/ knew his smile/ white above the mirror." to a chillingly understated effect.

Less spooky, perhaps more poignant are David Sutton's poems in his fourth collection, *Settlements* (Peterloo Poets, 2 Kelly Gardens, Calstock, Cornwall, PL18 9SA, £4.95). Sutton is very much a 'voice' poet in that you feel he is talking to you in diary-like fashion. Maybe something to do with the personal, reflective nature of his poems which focus on his children, the natural world and very much on the past. In 'Barna-Oddr', Sutton retells the story of the dissenting Viking who stood against the sport of "tossing children up and catching them/ on the points of spears." But

Sutton doesn't go in for the obvious choice of resurrecting an unsung hero, but instead uses his poem to lament the tendency of history to glorify the "brutish" aspects of the past.

Sutton is not alone in his interest in the past. Neal Mason even goes as far as to title his first collection *Excavations* (Peterloo Poets, £4.95) in his poetical homage into the past. But oddly enough, Mason writes much better in poems that aren't strictly to do with the past. His odes to a Roman sandal, a terracotta mouse (now at home in a museum) seem stifled, making bonds between the past and present that don't necessarily gel or make provocative reading. Yet when Mason writes about people, imagines himself characters, his poems breathe vibrantly. 'Spinster' is gripping in density of emotion. It begs to be read aloud and as an example of a man writing as a woman it is convincing and mercifully devoid of the usual patronising undercurrent. 'Eskimo Child' too reads authentically. He writes, as the child, of his wonder at the colour green in a world where white covers all with the "horizon bleached". Green is magical and exotic, belonging to the cities and the industrialised. By the time he reaches adulthood, he knows these 'green and pleasant lands' are the cause of his despair: "I wonder/ about trees and the colour green/ they traded for clouds of smoke./ My icy habitat shrinks, trapped/ by mining companies who burn/ the future as soon as the past/ my incredulous son wondering/ about the colour blue/ and the soot that falls like snow". Hopefully Mason will carry on writing with such range and skill.

Moving from lands of snow to New Caledonia, an island in the South Pacific, Nicholas Johnson's *Listening to the Stones* (The Many Press, 15 Norcott Road, London, N16 7BJ, £2.50) focuses on the conflicts that took place while he was there in the summer, 1988. The poems tell of the Kanaks and their struggle against French authorities who view the island as their overseas territor. You could almost call these 'docu-poems' since they inform of actual incidents of oppression as seen through the poet's eye. In 'A Holiday' he reveals how he and some Kanak friends run out of fuel for their car. The French settlers are unwilling to tell them where they can find diesel and where they do locate some, they "pass the army camp's/ honeyed fillets of wire: a soldier in calecon points/ his rifle at us, bored by/ the pacific." Documentary and poetry fuse well here. The scene is ambient with tension and a dreadful sense of quietness. The sense of oppression emerges here, as elsewhere, in a controlled manner made human and moving by the poetry which expresses it. A worthy and enlightening collection that makes you realise you don't know as much about what's going on in the world as you think you do.

Inside the forest, however there is something going on that William Oxley knows all about. *Forest Sequence* (Mammon Press, 12 Dartmouth Avenue, Bath, BA2 1AT, £1.50) takes on a detailed tour around the forest with an obvious accent on the trees that grow there. To make sure that you're not confused by this notion, trees photographed by Robert Palmer are added as an extra reminder. The trees themselves pose suggestively, with the odd close-up of a burly old trunk or two. Replete with lines such as "Autumn brings the thrust of pretty toadstools/ Coyly peering through dying grass/ Red-and-white spotted things tempting/ Us to pick them as we pass." *Forest Sequence* gives off the aura of an old school project, only without the naïve charm.

Daisies are smaller than trees but *Walks in a Daisy Chain* (Magenta, Middle Fold Farm, Colden, Heptonstall, Hebden Bridge, West Yorks, HX7 7PG, £6.25) are better than another stroll through *Forest Sequence*. Geraldine Monk's idea is for each poem to be read in series so that a 'daisy-chain' can be created from the last word(s) of a poem becoming the first word(s) of the next one. Each poem details with a singular character (41 in all) from barmaid to artist and vicar to chat-show host. If you follow her instructions you get some rewarding and fun results. In 'The Football Hooligan', the subject's final Neanderthal grunt "FACK YOU" becomes, in the more verbally considered poet's utterances "Fack you?/ Doesn't sound right/ like a rude rush of loutish worrystorms" in the subsequent poem.

Of more serious intent are the poems of Neil R MacCullum in *Portrait of a Calvinist* (Scots Independent, 51 Cowane Street, Stirling, FK8 1JW, £4.95). Written in Scots and English, the poems' tone is often subdued but always sincere. In 'Answering With an Echo',

MacCallum tells how, in Wales, he saw a street that "bore two names,/ one in English, the other running/ Side by side it/ Their own." This makes him think of his own lost tongue and the sadness of Gaelic "strewn/ Under so many headstones." Assured and able, MacCallum writes confidently as does W N Herbert in *Landfish* (Duncan of Jordanstone, College of Art, Dundee, £?). Pocket-sized but bumper packed, Herbert reels a strange tale set "thi Tay" that courses with vitality.

Pocket-sized too are the series of 7 Robin Moffat books (Palm Tree, Dowanside Lane, Glasgow, G12 9BZJ, £1.95-£2.95). On the back cover of each mini-collections, Moffat proudly proclaims the fact that he is a member of the Society of Authors and British Equity. This, however, does not imply that each member is a good poet. Moffat's little gems offer curious often childish view of the world. *Pillock* is home to poems concerned with the pains of unrequited love: "Angel had beauty/ she was perfect in feature/ age had failed/ to sag or line her" This sort of profundity is characteristic of Moffat's poems which tend to trip along in a world of their own.

Poems of Love and War (Lotus Editions Limited, 26 Tangier Road, Richmond, Surrey, TW10 5DW, £?) by Fran Barrault were written in Edinburgh during 1939-1945, although her illustrations have been completed recently. Early on sunflowers and bird song punctuate these compactly crafted poems, but their tone grows bleaker with the onset of war in poem, full of tension and despair. *Chiaroscuro* (Spendthrift publications, 31 Richmond Road, Cambridge, CB4 3PP, £4.95) consists of Louis J Rodrigues' own poems and translations of Anglo-Saxon, Catalan and Galician works. Rodrigues is obviously erudite, but could benefit from relaxing the authoritative tone which gives his poems a patriarchal feel.

Loftiness prevails in W G Shepard's *The Gifted Child* (The Many Press, 15 Norcott Road, London, N16 7BJ, £3.50). Alongside snatches of peace and beauty, marital discord and other forms of anger rear their heads in a collection which, though varied, lacks direction and a sense of conclusion. More experimental but just as inconclusive is Bob Cobbling's *Improvisation is a Dirty Word* (Magenta, £4.50). In fact, words don't appear at all except briefly on the contents page. Instead we are presented with page upon page of murky pictures which look as if a drunk (albeit a dextrous one) has been set loose on an unsuspecting photocopier. If there is a latent message here it remains entangled in its own obscurity with little hope for remission.

Three Epistles by S A Paterson and G J Cambridge (Longpark Resource Centre, Northcraig Road, Kilmarnock, Ayrshire, £?) offers welcome relief. As its title suggests the piece is written in the form of three letters between the authors. Paterson writes two in a terse, direct Scots and Cambridge the middle letter in verbose and grandiose English. The two contrast well in their forms of banter and make for an invigorating read.

A different landscape emerges in *Skimming the Soul* by Tariq Latif (Littlewood Arc, The Nanholme Centre, Shaw Wood Road, Todmorden, Lancs, OL14 6DA, £5.95). Now living in Manchester, many of Latif's poems are about the Pakistan of his childhood years. Precise images stalk the collection, especially in his Pakistan poems where faraway people and animals seem to there right in front of you: "Nothing disturbs the elephants'/ Communion. They must move on/ To where I'm not sure/ But they disappear, like/ pilgrims into the sun." Definitely a poet to watch.

Better established is Dand Gioia. The poems in *The Gods of Winter* (Peterloo Poets, £6.95) cover a varied emotional terrain. They display such empathy and thought that the word 'moving' is inadequate to describe them. Poems like 'Counting the Children' and 'All Souls" possess such power that they exist as definitions of poetry in simply being there. Only a read of Gioia's work can clarify my words further. **Sara Evans**

Catalogue

Duncan Glen's *The Poetry of the Scots* (Edinburgh UP, £25.00) is a near-comprehensive bibliography with notes on poets, and gets a black look (if not mark) for missing the huge selection of Naomi Mitchison's poetry in *Chapman* 50/51, though journals are usually acknowledged. There's little order to the notes, often casual, excessively personal, of length not proportionate to worth. And Joseph MacLeod was not merely 'Adam Drinan', ought to be in but isn't. Some editions of Gaelic poets have translations, which and how good isn't said. Nineteenth-century coverage is weak, W E Aytoun should not be unmentioned. Yet from an earlier age Alexander Montgomerie does much better than usual of late. Hopefully good correspondence will pour in, with improvements. Reviews can only make such points as the above, on what remains a major reference item.

The Minister's Cat (Aberdeen UP, £2.95) is a neat novelty, sundry Scots adjectives potentially applicable to a feline compiled by Hamish Whyte and supplied with *Concise Scots Dictionary* definitions and illuminated by Barbara Robertson; *More Scottish Poetry from MacGregor's Gathering* (BBC, £4.99) ed. MacG. and Mulrine collects Scots poems sent to the programme: an impressive hantle of popular Scots poetry. *Bothy Days and Nichts* (John Donald, £7.50) is a brief account with excellent photographs and some vivid ballads, well made by the Brechin local historian David G Adams. *Africa, contemporary poetry out of Africa* (European Association for the Promotion of Poetry, Blljde Inkomststraat 9, B-3000, Leuven, Belgium, n.p.) has versions in English, French and Dutch; introductions, a dozen poets featured, lots of information. Skoob publish a new verse translation of Rilke's *Sonnets to Orpheus* by Leslie Norris and Alan Keele (£5.99). Comment must be sacrificed to commend *Constructions* by Chris Bendon (Gomer Press, £7.95) a poet engaging with consonants or rough-edged images, and striking live rhythms. In a parade of modern period emblems and non-enthusiastic comments he masterfully eschews mere sentiment, disillusion, posed irony. "(useless to say it's what you *feel*)" he notes after imprinting one telling not understated image. More than useful that he's *real*!

Some adore Peter Greenaway's *Prospero's Books* (Chatto, £12.99) which like the film it parallels seems to bear out Faith Compton Mackenzie's view that the English prefer a watch's dismantled works to anything of beauty keeping time. Better some of the Scottish Variety Theatre of Vivien Devlin's *Kings, Queens and People's Palaces* (Polygon, £9.95), a collection of recollections on the populist side. Other Polygons: Andrew Murray Scott's biography *Alexander Trocchi, The Making of the Monster* (£14.95) is ill-written/edited unless the clumsy clinkers and dime-shocker prose are to echo beat rhythms. Trocchi was ingenious (not AMS's "genius"), as prolific in epithets as MacCaig but dreadfully dissociated as can be seen in *Invisible Insurrection of a Million Minds: A Trocchi Reader* (£8.95, ed. his biographer) where much beatness is projected, livelier than latter days, but a mess of disgust/fascination.

Eric Linklater's excessive professionalism won his novels a following they lost later. His son Andro refers to an awareness of the reality of darker powers: was his later bitterness a response to the loss of magical powers? *The Goose Girl and Other Stories* (ed Andro Linklater, Canongate £15.95) shows imaginative not just mere literary-strategic power. It might be worth being rude to his novels to emphasise the peculiarly limited but real genius here. Short Story enthusiasts may be drawn by *The Devil and Dr Tuberose*, 1991 and 19th volume in a Scottish Arts Council series: with the publisher now HarperCollins (£13.99), no longer the faintly dubious venture this short fiction annual once seemed. We'd be happier, however, if they acknowedged previous publication of the stories: the title story, by John Herdman, first appeared in *Chapman*.

The emeritus professor and one survivor at Edinburgh University's emaciated Russian dept, Dennis Ward and Mike Falchikov, translate impressive short stories by Viktor Nekrasov (1911-1987) *Postscripts* (Quartet, £12.95). This neglected writer, exiled for humanity rather than overt dissidence, offers balanced but honest understanding of pre-*glasnost* Soviet life, valid to the needed peaceful work of telling us that much said of USSR (RIP) is the West's way of remaining immune to self-knowledge.

Longer fiction treated more shortly: Gustav Meyrink's *The Angel of the West Window* (Daedalus, £18.99/£8.99), translated from German by Mike Mitchell of Stirling University, is a fantasy on the Elizabethan magus John Dee and the third in an impressive Meyrink list from the publisher. It would be unfair to compare Elspeth Barker's *O Caledonia*

(Hamish Hamilton, £14.99), its breathy style and echo of David 'Arcturus' Lindsay. I mention two new children's books, *Revenge of the Wildcat* by Griselda Gifford (£2.50), *The House in Hiding* by Elinor Lyn (£2.95), both Kelpies from Canongate. *Whithorn, Iona and Lindisfarne – a Celtic Saga*, by Andrew Paterson (St Andrew Press,£3.95) is informative at any level, Patrick, Ninian and co?

Edinburgh UP continue the valuable reprinting of Arnold's New History of Scotland with *Independence and Nationhood: Scotland 1306-1469* by Alexander Grant, and Jenny Wormald's *Court, Kirk and Community: 1470-1625* (£9.50 each). Alastair Gray's *Lanark* (Picador, £6.99) and Sorley MacLean's Collected Poems (Vintage £8.99) are both now in softback. Not due out quite yet (1999 is rumoured) are those whose past lives figure in Michael Turnbull's *The Edinburgh Graveyard Guide* (St Andrew Press, £4.95). Douglas Dunn's *Scotland, An Anthology* (HarperCollins £15.99) is a huge achievement with some ingenious choices. *The Jessie Kesson Omnibus* (Chatto, £16.00) collects 'White Bird', 'Apple Ripens', 'Another Time', 'Glitter of Mica': braw.

When the Tree Flowered (University of Nebraska Press, £6.95) is a welcome reprint of John Neihardt's 1951 Sioux cultural landmark. *The Faroe Islands* (John Murray, £10.95) extends a series by Liv Kjorsvik Schei and Gunnie Moberg, wider perspective on their previous Orkney and Shetland books. The text is full, Ms Moberg's photographs of their usual standard. *The Dundee Book, An Anthology of Living in the City* (ed Billy Kay, Mainstream, £14.99) has noble contributors, G W S Barrow, G Rosie, G Bruce &c, much more substance than usual inside a picture-book format cover. Steuart Campbell's *The Loch Ness Monster – The Evidence* (AUP, £5.95), a high-powered inquisition of the nadir silly-season topic, fascinates farcically. It was once declared fitting that a real and now-dead monster (no name, *nil nisi bonum*) had edited a previous snakebag of abusive and satirical verse. *I Have No Gun But I Can Spit* (Faber, £6.99) is ed. The Rt. Hon. Kenneth Baker, MP. As Iago sez, I "speak no word".

Notes on Contributors

Sebastian Barker, son of George Barker who died recently, is chairman of the Poetry Society in London.

Robert Calder has recently edited a collection of Karl M Abenheimer's essays (*Narcissism, Nihilism, Simplicity and Self*) and is preparing a book in 19th century Scottish philosophers.

Bernard Crick is Emeritus Professor of Politics at the University of London. Well-known and lively commentator on the Scottish political scene.

Simon Darragh, working backwards: plumber living in Greece, theatre technician, hospital porter, teacher, student of philosophy, music, science; born England.

Sara Evans reviews for the *Edinburgh Evening News* and is an editorial assistant with *Cencrastus* magazine.

Anne Frater: b. Lewis 1967. Studying for PhD at Glasgow University. Work published in *Gairm*; *Gairfish*; *An Aghaidh na Siorraidhead* and *An Anthology of Scottish Women Poets*.

Graham Fulton lives in Paisley. First major collection *Humouring the Iron Bar Man* published by Polygon in 1990. He's just completed work on his second.

Dairmid Gunn, a nephew of Neil Gunn, former naval officer and diplomat, with current interest in Scottish-Russian relations. Co-editor of *Neil Gunn's Country* and writer of introductions to Gunn's works.

Harvey Holton, b 1949, has lived in Fife for 15 years and Barra for 3. He has been published in *Finn* (Three Tigers), *Four Fife Poets* (AUP) and *New Makars*.

Jane Harris reviews fiction for STV's *Scottish Books* and is currently on a creative writing course in East Anglia.

Robert Alan Jamieson: Shetland-born novelist and poet, most recently *A Day at the Office* (Polygon) which is both poem and novel.

Michael Lister lectures in Information Management at the Scottish College of Testiles.

Neil MacCormick is Regius Professor of Public Law at Edinburgh University and prospective SNP candidate for Argyll & Bute.

Ian McCulloch: Glasgow painter, exhibited widely, with work in many major collections including ICA, Saatchi Collections.

Margery McCulloch is a Scottish literature scholar trying to survive in a macho academic world. She is an Open University tutor and visiting lecturer at Glasgow and Strathclyde universities.

Julie Morrice is theatre critic of *Scotland on Sunday* and daughter of the poet Ken Morrice.

Peter Mowat: I write under a full moon/ in the open air/ as far from civilisation/ as the extension cable/ from my flickering word screen will allow/ until the shilling runs out.

Donald Munro, 29ish, from a Lewis family, writes poetry and prose in Gaelic and English, currently working on a book of Finnish folktales for children. Lives in Argyll with wife, son and two demanding cats.

Tom Nairn: writer & journalist working at STV. Books include *The Breakup of Britain* (1977) and *The Enchanted Glass* (1988); TV projects include STV's film of the latter (1990), and *Disunited Kingdom* (1987).

Richard Price's study of Neil M Gunn is published by Edinburgh University Press. He is an editor of *Gairfish* and *Verse*, and a curator of Modern British Collections at the British Libary in London.

Alison Prince lives on the Isle of Arran. She has written many a children's book and, more recently, two adult novels and a book on creative thinking.

Tom Scott is long established as a poet of international reputation, writing in Scots and English. He specialises in long poems like *The Tree* and *The Ship*; lives in Edinburgh.

Fred Urquhart is well known as a novelist and short story writer. He has recently moved back to Scotland and now lives in Musselburgh.